Unleashing Empowerment and Resilience:
A Proven Framework for Healing, Strength, and Lasting Legacy

Dr. Lila Elliott

Preface

Resilience Rising: A Movement for Every Trailblazer

Welcome to a movement! An unapologetic call to unleash your resilience and create a legacy that resonates through generations. I'm Dr. Lila Elliott, and after nineteen years of supporting warriors as a social worker, I developed "Unleashing Empowerment and Resilience: A Proven Framework for Healing, Strength, and Lasting Legacy." This framework aims to ignite the passion of every professional, whether in offices, homes, classrooms, nonprofit organizations, or hospitals.

This self-help manual is designed for you, whether you are leading teams, shaping young minds, or building communities. It especially honors Black women, whose strength inspires us all. My Empowerment and Resilience Framework (ERF) isn't just a theoretical concept; it's a proven guide based on real stories of triumph over trauma, systemic bias, and doubt. In the pages ahead, you'll discover actionable strategies that not only heal and empower but also ignite leadership from a place of hard-earned strength, transforming personal pain into collective power.

Unleashing Empowerment and Resilience

Table of Contents

Preface iii

INTRODUCTION vii

CHAPTER 1: The Unspoken Wounds 11

CHAPTER 2: Double Bind: Racism and Gender Bias 29

CHAPTER 3: Education as a Lifeline 41

CHAPTER 4: Theories that Heal 53

CHAPTER 5: Building the Framework 63

CHAPTER 6: The Power of Culturally Rooted Support 73

CHAPTER 7: From Surviving to Thriving 83

CHAPTER 8: Legacy and Leadership 93

Acknowledgement 103

References 105

ABOUT THE AUTHOR 107

INTRODUCTION

From a Vision to a Victory: The ERF Was Born

The Birth of the Empowerment and Resilience Framework:
your pain is not your endpoint; it's the spark that builds an
unbreakable legacy.
– Dr. Lila Elliott

Welcome to Unleashing Empowerment and Resilience: A
Proven Framework for Healing, Strength, and Lasting
Legacy. This isn't just another self-help manual; it's a call to
action, a fire to ignite your strength, and a blueprint to create
legacies that ripple through time.

At the heart of this movement is my Empowerment and
Resilience Framework (ERF), a powerful and proven tool I
developed during my doctoral journey. This framework is
designed to transform pain into power, doubt into
determination, and survival into thriving. Its roots trace back
to my own story of resilience.

As a Black woman, I have navigated paths shaped by trauma,
with childhood wounds that lingered like uninvited guests. I
have experienced the sting of systemic racism and sexism,
which often made me feel like I had to be twice as good to
get half as far. Yet education became my revolution, an
awakening that turned adversity into purpose and equipped
me to rise beyond the barriers meant to contain me.

During my doctoral studies, my capstone project
(dissertation) became my proving ground. I wanted to create
something meaningful that resonated with my soul and could
serve others.

That's when the ERF was born. The ERF emerged as a combination of three influential theories: Black Feminist Theory, Trauma-Informed Care Theory, and the Academic Resilience Theory. As a Black woman, a survivor of trauma, and someone who values education, these theories resonate deeply with me. They also provide essential tools for empowerment for everyone.

Black Feminist Theory serves as the foundation for the ERF. It encourages us to view the world through the experiences of Black women, acknowledging our intersectional identities shaped by race, gender, and class. This perspective **empowered me to stand rooted in my identity and lead with cultural authority, not apology.** It also compels all professionals to recognize and validate the unique stories of those they serve, particularly Black women.

Trauma-Informed Care Theory serves as a safe harbor, as it recognizes the profound emotional, mental, and physical impacts of trauma. It creates environments where healing **is expected, not excused, where restoration replaces shame. It equips anyone touched by pain, from early trauma to professional burnout, with practical tools to rebuild with strength and self-respect.**

Academic Resilience Theory acts as the driving force, illustrating how education, whether in a classroom, office, or home, can be a lifeline for overcoming adversity. It emphasizes the importance of building networks, setting goals, and finding strength through learning, regardless of one's field. **These theories converge within the ERF to give professionals, from clinicians to educators, corporate leaders to parents, a clear, actionable roadmap for cultivating true resilience.**

My mission was clear: to create a framework that was not only academic but also actionable. One that can be implemented in mental health settings, hospitals, schools, universities, offices, and even living rooms. The ERF is built on three core values: dignity, pride, and self-determination. It aims to validate everyone's worth, celebrate cultural strengths, and empower individuals to chart their own paths.

For Black women, this framework serves as a love letter to our resilience, recognizing the additional burden of the systemic challenges we face. For all professionals, it is a universal call to transform personal healing into collective empowerment. This self-help manual is not just meant to be read; it is designed to be actively used and applied.

Each chapter is packed with stories, strategies, and exercises to bring the ERF to life in your world. You'll meet composites of the warriors I've walked with over my 19 years as a mental health professional. They are everyday visionaries; people who've faced bias, carried trauma, and still dared to dream. Whether you lead a team, teach a classroom, or nurture a family, you'll gain powerful tools, from practical workshops to soulful rituals, that cultivate unshakable resilience. The ERF is your blueprint to transform pain into power, not just for yourself but for those you lead, teach, or love. It's time to rise, to build, and to answer the call of the legacy you're destined to leave. Your legacy isn't just waiting, it's calling. Let's unleash it together with the Dr. Lila Effect™ | Architect of Legacy™.

Write a brief vision of what empowerment looks like to you.

CHAPTER 1: The Unspoken Wounds

"Unspoken wounds don't just linger—they lie. Call them out and unleash the power to rewrite your story." –
Dr. Lila Elliott

At 2:14 p.m., I am returning a hotline call. The veteran, 42, speaks with a voice like gravel, rough and weathered, carrying the weight of years spent shouting over gunfire and swallowing silence: "They sound like I'm going to assume they are already a statistic." I freeze while listening to him, my mind drifting back to my nine-year-old self in my room, escaping the chaos of my childhood home, where verbal arguments echoed around me. That wound? It told me that silence keeps you safe. "This is a safe space for you to be yourself, free from judgment," I say, softly, "I am listening to you. I hear you. Let's address what they're not saying." He exhales his first real breath in minutes.

We outline his dignity on the call synopsis form; by 2:41, his suicide plan turns into a follow-up appointment. The wound has been identified, and the chain has been broken. Why? Dr. Lila Elliott used her effective and practical skills in crisis intervention.

Break the Silence, Ignite Your Strength

As a girl, growing up Black in a world such as ours felt overwhelming. I felt deep wounds that I couldn't express. This included family chaos, the pain of being overlooked, and the pressure to always be "strong." Sound familiar?

Whether you're a supervisor managing work life stress, a teacher inspiring young minds, a nurse on the front lines, or a parent holding everything together, we all bear unspoken wounds. For Black women, these wounds are compounded by systemic racism and sexism, but the impact of trauma, emotional, mental, and physical, affects every professional's life. As a social worker, I have witnessed this in professional environments, classrooms, and therapy sessions. My ERF is designed to help you identify these wounds boldly and transform pain into power. This chapter serves as our wake-up call: let's heal, connect, and create legacies that drive change.

The Birth of the ERF: A Personal and Scholarly Revolution

Imagine this: I'm deep into my doctoral journey at the University of Kentucky (UK), a Black woman carrying the weight of my childhood trauma, family chaos, systemic racism, and the pressure to be "twice as good" just to be recognized. Education has been my lifeline and my rebellion against a world that attempts to dim my light. However, while working with patients at Riverside, veterans at the Veterans Affairs (VA), and students at UK, I noticed a significant gap. Professionals, therapists, teachers, executive leadership, and parents were eager for ways to foster resilience that felt authentic, not just theoretical. This realization led to the creation of the ERF during my doctoral research; it became a labor of love aimed at developing a framework that transforms pain into power for everyone, especially with a fierce focus on Black women.

Black Feminist Theory: The Heart of the ERF

Black Feminist Theory, as articulated by Patricia Hill Collins (2000), serves as the foundation of the ERF, focusing on the lived experiences of Black women. As a Black woman, my voice was too often dismissed; my presence questioned before I even spoke. This theory provided me with the language to articulate my struggle with intersectionality and allowed me to recognize my cultural pride as a source of strength.

In my capstone project, I utilized Hill Collins' (2000) framework to argue that the unique socio-cultural narratives of Black women, shaped by systemic oppression, deserve recognition in the contexts of healing and empowerment. The ERF employs this perspective to affirm the strengths of Black women in professional settings, from boardrooms to classrooms, while encouraging all professionals to honor diverse identities. From classrooms to counseling rooms, I lead with this truth: **"Your story is your Power. Own it."**

Trauma-Informed Care Theory: The Safe Harbor

Trauma-Informed Care Theory, grounded in the principles set forth by Substance Abuse and Mental Health Services Administration [SAMHSA] (2014), serves as a safe harbor at the ERF. Through my work with clients, including survivors of abuse, veterans with post-traumatic stress disorder (PTSD), and students struggling with self-doubt, I have learned that trauma is not just a story; it is a burden carried in both the body and the mind. SAMHSA's research indicates that the impact of trauma is universal, but for Black women, it is exacerbated by systemic stressors such as racism (Gillum, 2019).

In my doctoral research, I emphasized the importance of creating safe and empowering spaces to prevent re-traumatization, a practice I integrate into therapy at Riverside and in my training sessions for professionals (SAMHSA, 2014). The ERF puts these principles into practice: in hospitals, I educate colleagues to conduct gentle check-ins; in schools, I guide teachers in fostering trust. It's essential to convey the message, "You're safe here," to everyone, from executives to parents.

Academic Resilience Theory: The Fire of Learning

Academic Resilience Theory, as outlined by Martin and Marsh (2006), serves as the foundation of the ERF. Education has been my escape from pain and my pathway to purpose. In my research, I referenced this theory to illustrate how both formal and informal learning foster resilience through supportive networks and personal determination (Martin & Marsh, 2006).

For Black women, education acts as a rebellion against systemic barriers, but it is also a vital lifeline for everyone (O'Shea & Stone, 2014). I have witnessed this in students at UK, who push through self-doubt, as well as in veterans at the VA, who learn new skills to reclaim their power. The ERF embodies this concept across various settings. Whether it's executive leader's upskilling, teachers mentoring, or parents educating their children, demonstrating that education can ignite universal resilience.

Why these three theories?

Because they're *my* story. Black Feminist Theory spoke to my soul as a Black woman, honoring the intersection of race, gender, and class that shapes our fight. Trauma-Informed Care Theory mirrored my work helping clients heal from wounds without shame, creating safe spaces in therapy rooms and classrooms. Academic Resilience Theory was my intimate message to education, the tool that lifted me and countless others through adversity. I didn't just pick these theories; they chose me, reflecting my truth as a survivor, scholar, and advocate. The ERF became my way to weave them into a single, actionable blueprint that works everywhere. Hospitals, schools, offices, homes, because resilience isn't confined to one space.

Why the ERF? A Framework for All Settings

The ERF was created to address existing gaps. During my research, I observed how universal approaches frequently neglect the specific cultural and systemic realities faced by Black women (Erving et al., 2021; Moorosi et al., 2018).

Resilience is universal; every professional must learn to rise after the fall and lead from their scars, not despite them. The core values of the ERF: dignity, pride, and self-determination, transcend boundaries, adapting seamlessly across every context.

In mental health settings, I apply it to guide trauma therapy; in schools, I use it to empower educators and students; in workplaces, I foster inclusive leadership; and at home, it helps to strengthen family bonds. Research supports its effectiveness: culturally specific frameworks improve resilience by addressing unique stressors while bringing together diverse groups (Bertaux & Anderson, 2001; Chance, 2022).

The ERF in Action: A Movement for Legacy

The ERF is not just a theory; it's a movement that I have truly embraced. While counseling veterans, I witness their trauma transform into strength within safe and affirming spaces. In my teaching at UK, I see students embracing their cultural pride and setting ambitious goals. In corporate spaces, I challenge teams to build resilience cultures; spaces where inclusion isn't an initiative, but a norm. My capstone project demonstrated the ERF's ability to heal and empower, particularly for Black women, by incorporating research-backed strategies (Hamilton-Mason et al., 2009). This framework is effective; its power lies in truth, born from real stories, forged through pain, and proven by transformation.

As you explore this self-help manual, know that the ERF is more than a framework. It's a call to rise, to heal, and to lead with purpose. It is intended for every professional who is ready to heal, lead, and leave a lasting impact. To Black women, it serves as a billet-doux celebrating your resilience. For everyone else, it is an invitation to build something unstoppable. Let's do this journey together.

Tamara's Therapy Truth (Private Practice)

Tamara faced the emotional challenges stemming from childhood verbal abuse, which resulted in chronic migraines and self-doubt. This made her experience intense burnout as a therapist, leading her to question her ability to help others. This struggle was further complicated by the systemic bias that often silenced the voices of Black women in her field.

Tamara's Therapy Truth

Tamara, a 35-year-old Black therapist in Detroit inner city, had built her practice on helping families navigate crises, but she was also grappling with her own struggles. Growing up in a home where her mother's constant criticism pierced her like knives, Tamara often heard, "You're never enough, girl." To keep the peace, Tamara learned to shrink herself, to survive by disappearing. But that pain didn't stay behind; it seeped into her work, showing up in migraines and moments of quiet exhaustion.

As a Black woman in social work, she encountered additional challenges, such as colleagues questioning her expertise on cultural trauma and clients assuming she was "tough enough" to endure everything without breaking down. The "stay strong" code she grew up with conflicted with her professional obligation to show vulnerability. Isolation became her norm. She skipped lunches, powered through exhaustion, and questioned whether a wounded healer could ever lead others to wholeness.

One afternoon, after dealing with a particularly challenging case involving a young Black girl who had experienced similar abuse, Tamara reached her breaking point. Tears streamed down her face, and her hands shook in her office. At that moment, she decided to reach out to my ERF group at Riverside, a space I created for professionals like her to discuss trauma without fear of judgment.

In the circle, surrounded by a diverse group of healers, she shared her story for the first time: the nights she hid under her bed as a child and how the echoes of criticism still resonate in her migraines today. The group listened attentively as I guided her through a body scan, helping her connect her physical pain to those emotional scars. The experience was raw, filled with tears, nods of understanding, and even a shared laugh when someone said, "We all carry that backpack, sis."

Tamara's breakthrough came when she realized her trauma wasn't a weakness. It was a call to power, an inheritance she could choose to rewrite. She began journaling daily, transforming her pain into purpose, and with time, her migraines softened as her confidence returned.

Tamara's story reminds us that healing isn't about erasing the past; it's about reclaiming the power it tried to take from her.

ERF Practical Application Solutions:

- **Dignity Affirmation Ritual:** Begin each day with a 5-minute mirror talk, affirming, "My wounds do not define me, they design my legacy." This practice draws from Black Feminist Theory to honor your identity as a Black woman, transforming self-doubt into daily empowerment for therapy sessions or client interactions.

- **Trauma-Informed Body Mapping:** Use a notebook to sketch where pain resides in your body, labeling those areas with emotions and cultural strengths, such as ancestral resilience. This approach incorporates Trauma-Informed Care Theory to establish safe self-checks that help reduce physical symptoms and enhance mental clarity for Black women dealing with professional stress.

- **Resilience Goal Chain:** Connect one small weekly goal to your trauma narrative, such as "Share one vulnerability in a meeting." This practice uses Academic Resilience Theory to promote self-determination, creating a chain of accomplishments that shifts your experience from mere survival to thriving, empowering you to architect a legacy of strength.

Sofia's Classroom Clarity (High School)

Sofia struggled with anxiety due to her parents' tumultuous divorce, manifesting as stomach knots and mental fog. The pressure to "be strong" culturally compounded her feelings, leading to overwork and burnout, which hindered her ability to effectively support her students.

Sofia is a 28-year-old Mexican American high school counselor in Los Angeles. She grew up in a family where emotions were often suppressed, guided by the mantra "familia first, no complaints." Her parents' divorce when she was twelve left her with a constant knot in her stomach, a physical reminder of the chaos, yelling, and fear of abandonment she experienced during that time. In her busy high school office, surrounded by teens dealing with their own challenges, that knot tightens during crisis counseling. This pressure causes her to second-guess her advice and pushes her to work through her exhaustion, as she strives to prove that she is "strong enough."

As a Latina in education, she faced additional bias, with administrators assuming she was better suited for "diversity" roles rather than leadership positions. This assumption amplified her self-doubt, leading to late nights spent preparing sessions, skipping meals, and feeling isolated from colleagues who didn't understand the cultural pressures she faced to hold everything together.

One day, a young Latina female student broke down about her own family split, mirroring Sofia's pain so closely that she felt frozen, her stomach churning. This experience prompted her to sign up for my ERF workshop for educators, a space where I blend theory with practical insights. In the group, she opened up about her divorce, connecting her struggles to unresolved trauma.

I guided a reflection exercise, using the ERF to help her articulate her pain and link it to her cultural resilience, recalling how her abuela's stories of survival had inspired her. The room was filled with teachers from diverse backgrounds, many of whom shared similar experiences, fostering a bond that made Sofia feel truly seen.

By acknowledging her wounds, she began a daily breathing ritual that eased her anxiety and transformed her approach to counseling. She started student groups focused on emotional check-ins, allowing students like that young female to find their voices. Sofia's newfound clarity turned her classroom into a sanctuary, demonstrating that healing is not a solitary journey; it's a shared legacy.

ERF Practical Application Solutions:

- **Pride-Infused Journaling:** Dedicate 10 minutes each night to journal about your cultural strengths (e.g., "My Latina heritage teaches endurance"). Use Black Feminist Theory to reclaim your identity, helping Black women in education transition from overwork to balanced leadership as a proven path to resilience.
- **Safe Space Creation Kit:** Build a "resilience corner" in your workspace with calming items (such as a candle and a photo of your ancestors). Apply Trauma-Informed Care Theory principles to foster self-determination, allowing Black women to pause and

reframe trauma in high-stress environments like classrooms.

- **Mentorship Goal Ladder:** Partner with a mentor to create "ladder rungs" for small achievements (e.g., "Delegate one task weekly"). Use Academic Resilience Theory to transform doubt into action, empowering Black women to embrace their legacy of thriving in professional roles.

Wei's Veteran Awakening (Veterans Affairs)

Wei struggled with PTSD from combat and family neglect. He experienced chest tightness and mental isolation, worsened by a cultural stoicism that suppressed emotions and strained relationships. This led to sleepless nights and avoidance of support.

Wei is a 42-year-old Chinese American veteran living in Virginia. He comes from a family where emotions were not openly expressed; his father often said, "Don't show weakness," a lesson rooted in their immigrant struggles. Combat experiences intensified this mindset, leaving him with PTSD-related nightmares and a persistent tightness in his chest. Group therapy often felt like a battlefield to him. At the VA, where I lead ERF sessions, Wei typically sat in the back with his arms crossed, his mind racing with feelings of isolation. The issue ran deep: his cultural upbringing, emphasizing stoicism, conflicted with his deep-seated need for connection. This internal struggle led to sleepless nights, strained family relationships, and a fear of vulnerability that prevented him from reaching out to fellow veterans. As an Asian American in a predominantly white group, he often felt overlooked, with his trauma dismissed as "just stress," which further fueled his doubts about the healing process.

During one session, a story shared by a Black veteran about family neglect resonated deeply with Wei, bringing back memories of his father's absence. After the group, he chose to stay behind, and I used ERF to gently guide him through a body scan. He became aware of the tightness in his body as a protective response to trauma. Identifying it as a reaction to adversity, rather than a sign of failure, marked a pivotal moment for him. We incorporated Academic Resilience Theory to outline his support system, which included a buddy system with a fellow Asian veteran. When he shared his story in the next group session, tears flowed for the first time. The room responded with nods and hugs, helping to break his sense of isolation. In his daily life, Wei now practices a two-minute gratitude list each night, reframing his pain as a source of strength, which has helped reduce his nightmares. He has taken on a mentoring role for new veterans, teaching them ERF tools and transforming his own awakening into a legacy of brotherhood. His journey illustrates that healing is a cultural, personal, and shared experience; no one fights alone.

ERF Practical Application Solutions:

- **Self-Determination Vision Board:** Create a board with images of cultural heroes and personal goals (e.g., "Connect with family weekly"), using Black Feminist Theory to affirm Black women's intersectional strength, shifting from isolation to empowered connections in veterans' groups or daily life.
- **Dignity Breath Work**: Practice 5-minute breaths focusing on "I am worthy of healing," applying Trauma-Informed Care Theory to build safe inner spaces, helping Black women release physical trauma symptoms like tightness, as a birthright to architect legacies of peace.
- **Resilience Network Web:** Map 5 supports (e.g., "Call a vet buddy daily"), drawing on Academic Resilience Theory to foster grit, empowering Black women to

weave trauma into a web of strength for thriving in professional and personal settings.

Sarah's Salon Sanctuary (Hair Salon)

Sarah felt drained from an alcoholic parent's legacy, with backaches and emotional numbness, avoiding deep connections and questioning her business, leading to low self-worth and strained client relationships.

Sarah is a 30-year-old white hairstylist living in Nashville. Coming from a small-town family, she learned to navigate her father's drunken rages by numbing her feelings to survive. This emotional numbness followed her into her work at the salon, where long hours resulted in persistent backaches, serving as a physical reminder of the tension she carried. Although her clients loved her haircuts, she kept conversations superficial, fearing that showing vulnerability would disrupt her "happy" facade. As a business owner in a diverse neighborhood, Sarah witnessed her Black and Latina clients dealing with their own traumas. However, she felt unprepared to connect with them, which led to feelings of isolation and self-doubt regarding her role as a community staple.

The situation worsened when a regular client, a Black woman, shared her story of abuse, which mirrored Sarah's pain so closely that Sarah froze, her back seizing up. That night, she signed up for my ERF community talk, a space for everyday professionals to heal. In the group, surrounded by hairstylists, nurses, and teachers, Sarah named her trauma for the first time: the nights spent hiding in her closet and the way it had turned her body into a vault of unspoken hurt.

I guided a reflection using the ERF, connecting her backaches to the emotional armor she had built. We explored cultural storytelling to release that pain. The room resonated with similar experiences. A Black stylist spoke of the weight of racism, and Sarah felt the connection. Her breakthrough came when she integrated this framework into her salon through "story time" during appointments, creating a safe space for clients to "open up."

One Black client shared her tale of overcoming neglect, which inspired Sarah to start journaling her own pain each night. This practice eased her physical aches and transformed her salon into a sanctuary. Clients returned, drawn by the healing atmosphere, and Sarah's self-worth soared. She even started a local group for women entrepreneurs. Her story reminds us that healing often lies in the everyday, turning wounds into wisdom.

ERF Practical Application Solutions:

- **Pride Legacy Tree:** Create a tree illustration with roots representing cultural strengths, such as "Community bonds from my heritage." Use Black Feminist Theory to celebrate the intersectional power of Black women, transforming emotional numbness into vibrant legacy-building, whether in salons/barber shops or homes.

- **Safe Story Circle:** Gather 2-3 trusted friends for weekly sharing sessions, utilizing Trauma-Informed Care Theory to establish boundaries, such as "no advice, just listening." This approach helps Black women alleviate physical discomfort caused by trauma, serving as a well-researched pathway to both physical and emotional freedom.

- **Goal Resilience Ladder:** Progress through "rungs" of small actions, such as "Share one story each week." This concept draws on Academic Resilience Theory to foster self-determination, empowering Black women to transform low self-worth into thriving relationships and professional success.

Research-Based Insight: The Proven Science of Trauma's Grip

The ERF, as a proven framework from my doctoral capstone at UK, addresses trauma as overwhelming experiences that linger, reshaping self-perception and manifesting in emotional, mental, and physical ways, particularly for Black women, where childhood adversities are compounded by racial and gender-based challenges (Bertaux & Anderson, 2001; Erving et al., 2021; Gillum, 2019). The capstone's Systematic Literature Review (SLR) Paper reveals that early pains, like familial disruptions or discrimination, lead to mental health issues such as depression, anxiety, and attachment insecurities, while cultural expectations to "stay strong" silence pain and amplify overachievement as a coping mechanism (Chance, 2022; Hamilton-Mason et al., 2009). The Conceptual Paper (CP) highlights how trauma affects the body and mind, with structural brain changes from adverse experiences contributing to emotional regulation difficulties and cognitive processing issues (Erving et al., 2021; Luthar et al., 2000). For Black women, the Practice Application Paper (PAP) emphasizes the compounded effects of racial and gender-based challenges, such as institutional racism and inadequate support, perpetuating cycles of disadvantage (Hill Collins, 2000; Moorosi et al., 2018). The capstone's introduction notes that despite these barriers, Black women often surpass peers in educational attainment, channeling trauma into drive, though this can lead to burnout and imposter syndrome (Martin & Marsh, 2006; O'Shea & Stone, 2014). The ERF integrates Black Feminist Theory to validate these unique socio-cultural narratives, fostering resilience by turning vulnerability into strength across professions, as evidenced by the capstone's call for trauma-informed curricula and mentorship to break intergenerational cycles (Hooks, 1981; SAMHSA, 2014). This research-backed approach ensures the ERF is not just a theory but a practical tool for professionals to support healing in diverse settings, from therapy to classrooms, empowering Black women to rewrite their endings through academic and personal triumph (Hauff et al., 2017; Xu, 2024).

Practical Strategies: Tools to Name and Transform Trauma

Guiding clients at VA, Riverside, and teaching at UK, I have developed strategies that are effective for professionals in any field. These strategies are rooted in the ERF's core values—dignity, pride, and self-determination—and are designed to make naming trauma a daily practice:

1. **Simplify Trauma Talk:** Frame it as "the heavy stuff that sticks, like a backpack you didn't choose." I tell clients, "It's not weakness; it's life. Let's unpack it." In team huddles or personal rituals, this approach opens doors without shame, especially for Black women who carry systemic burdens.
2. **Spark Courageous Conversations:** Ask, "What early moment still shapes your choices?" I use this in trainings to build trust across cultures, validating the layered experiences of Black women while connecting with all professionals.
3. **Honor Cultural Layers:** For Black women, acknowledge, "Your strength against systemic odds is epic." For all, affirm unique struggles to foster empathy. I apply this in veteran groups to bridge cultural gaps.
4. **Feel the Body's Story:** Lead a 3-minute body scan where participants notice tension and link it to their emotions. I guide this exercise in therapy to make healing tangible, helping to reduce physical symptoms like migraines.
5. **Normalize Resilience:** Remind teams, "We all carry scars; they fuel our strength." In my university courses,

this message unites diverse professionals, transforming trauma into collective empowerment.

6. **Daily Integration:** Conclude each day with a "wound-to-strength" note, reflecting on what pain surfaced and how it made you stronger. I assign this practice to clients in high-stress roles, such as teaching or finance, to encourage positive mindset shifts.

The First Step to Healing

Healing starts with courage, the courage to face your truth head-on. In my practice, I have witnessed professionals transform when they stop concealing their pain. Whether you are a Black woman in corporate America or a high school teacher, take a moment today to recognize one wound, whether big or small.

This isn't about 'fixing' yourself. It's about owning your story. This is where the journey of ERF begins, transforming silence into strength. From my capstone's SLR, we understand that early adversities, such as family disruptions, can have lasting effects. However, the PAP demonstrates that workshops like "Empower, Educate, Elevate" can help you create safe spaces. Your first step in this journey lays the foundation for your legacy; embrace it.

Activity Exercises:
Claiming Your Strength

Trauma Timeline: Reflect on three significant moments in your life and consider how they have shaped your beliefs today. Take a moment to map these experiences. Be honest; there is no judgment here. Additionally, reflect on one positive change that has resulted from those experiences.

Body Check-In

Journal About: "Where's stress in my body? What emotions are tied to it?" Sketch it out for clarity.

Cultural Story Share:

Write about how your identity influences the challenges you face. Share this reflection in a safe space, such as a personal journal or with a trusted friend.

Resilience Reframe:

Identify one way in which your trauma has made you stronger (for example, "I'm a survivor"). Transform this insight into an affirmation for tomorrow.

Reflection Prompts:

1. What childhood moment continues to influence your decisions, and how can you respond to it with kindness?
2. How does your body signal stress, and what message is it trying to convey?
3. What cultural messages have shaped the way you handle pain, and how can you redefine them?
4. When have you felt most confident in your professional role, and how can you harness that confidence now?
5. How can you create a safe space for someone else to express their wounds?
6. What is one truth you've been afraid to admit, and how would acknowledging it set you free?
7. How has trauma influenced your leadership style, and what changes can you make?
8. What strength from your past can you celebrate today?

Final Reflection Question: In what ways can acknowledging your unspoken wounds today encourage someone in my circle to do the same?

CHAPTER 2: Double Bind: Racism and Gender Bias

"The double bind tries to chain you—shatter it with your unyielding light and unapologetic truth." – Dr. Lila Elliott

A white student rolled her eyes and asked, "Why do we keep bringing race into the policing data?" I paused for a moment and thought of Hill Collins (2000). I explained that when I was at Riverside's intake bay at 41, a white supervisor told me, "Don't act Black!" That wasn't just feedback; it was a double bind. I was being told to either show up as brilliant or to play it safe, but not both.

The class fell silent. The Black cadet in row three uncrossed his arms. We shifted to the ERF slide, emphasizing that dignity means having a steady voice, pride means maintaining a straight posture, and self-determination means understanding that your statistics are just data and not your destiny. The essay scores improved the following week; the bind had loosened. Clearly, Dr. Lila Elliott had effectively utilized her ERF practical skills.

Smashing the Chains

I have stood in rooms where my voice as a Black woman was dismissed, my ideas questioned, and my presence underestimated. Not because of a lack of value, but because bias was in the room before I was. That double bind of racism and sexism is a struggle that Black women face daily, but bias affects us all in some way. Whether you're leading a company, helping clients in a crisis, teaching the next generation, or caring for patients, you know what it feels like to be undervalued. The difference lies in how we choose to rise above it and reshape the systems that keep it alive.

I've seen Black women code-switch just to be heard, educators battle daily to assert authority, and corporate leaders in finance fight twice as hard to prove what they already are: exceptional. This chapter provides you with the tools and language to articulate that struggle, explore its impact on your self-worth and opportunities, and rise above it with the ERF. Based on my capstone's SLR paper, we understand that systemic barriers like institutional racism exacerbate the trauma that affects Black women's ambition. However, the CP demonstrates that the ERF's Black Feminist Theory can validate these experiences. Let's work together to break these chains. Your legacy can start now.

Jennette's Corporate Stand (Corporate America)

Jennette faced microaggressions, being labeled "sassy" for speaking up, which led to code-switching exhaustion, insomnia, and self-doubt that stalled her career and amplified burnout as a Black woman in a predominantly white field.

Jennette is a 46-year-old Black Human Resource Director navigating New York's fast-paced corporate environment. She has worked her way up from an entry-level recruiter, but she constantly faces the dual challenges of racism and sexism. In meetings, her ideas are often dismissed as "too aggressive," while male colleagues receive praise for displaying the same assertiveness. This has forced her to engage in code-switching; softening her tone, hiding her natural curls under wigs, and smiling through her struggles just to fit in. The emotional toll has been significant: she suffers from insomnia, which leaves her exhausted, and self-doubt creeps in, making her question whether she is "executive material."

Additionally, a lingering fear of losing her job looms over her, as systemic bias adds extra pressure for her to prove herself twice as much. Gender norms further complicate her experience, often labeling her as "intimidating."

During one performance review, her boss suggested she "tone it down," which ignited a wave of frustration within her. That moment marked a turning point, and she decided to join my ERF corporate training, a space designed to help professionals address bias. In this group, Jennette shared her story, reflecting on how childhood expectations to "be strong" collided with the discrimination she faces in the workplace.

I facilitated a reflection using the ERF, highlighting the double bind as a systemic issue rather than a personal one. We practiced advocacy scripts, and Jennette role-played her response: "My passion drives results, let's focus on that." The room, filled with diverse executives, shared similar challenges, creating a sense of connection.

Jennette's breakthrough came from integrating the ERF into her daily routine. Morning affirmations like "My Black womanhood is my superpower" eased her insomnia and strengthened her presence. She became a mentor to a young Black intern, modeling how to navigate workplace bias with confidence.

In meetings, she spoke unapologetically, championing diversity policies that reshaped her company. Today, clients seek her out for her authentic leadership. Jennette's story isn't just personal; it's a blueprint for breaking barriers for women of color across corporate America.

ERF Practical Application Solutions:

- **Unapologetic Voice Ritual:** Engage in daily mirror affirmations with phrases like "My truth breaks chains." This practice is rooted in Black Feminist Theory and aims to help Black women reclaim their identities. It empowers them to move from code-switching to authentic leadership in corporate settings, as your doctoral birthright to empowerment.
- **Bias Boundary Builder:** Set "no-go" limits for

microaggressions (e.g., "Redirect conversations with facts"), using Trauma-Informed Care Theory to protect emotional health, empowering Black women to ease insomnia from stress, and architect legacies of self-protection.

- **Ambition Ally Network:** Connect with 2-3 mentors for weekly check-ins. Drawing on the principles of Academic Resilience Theory, this network fosters self-determination and helps transform self-doubt into career successes for Black women in high-stakes fields.

Priya's Finance Fight (Finance)

Priya was passed over for promotions due to stereotypes about her quiet demeanor. This caused her mental fatigue, anxiety, and a fear of speaking up, which limited her contributions and eroded her ambition.

Priya is a 32-year-old Indian American analyst working in the competitive finance sector in Chicago. She immigrated to the United States as a child with her family, learning the value of humility to navigate challenges. However, in her firm, that humility has worked against her. Her superiors have overlooked her for promotions, mistakenly perceiving her soft-spoken nature as a sign of being "not leader material." On top of that, gender bias has compounded her struggle with self-doubt.

As a result, she experiences mental fatigue from overanalyzing every email, enduring anxiety knots in her stomach before meetings, and developing a growing fear of speaking up, which keeps her ideas unshared and stalls her career progression. As an Indian American woman, Priya finds herself in a double bind: perceived as a "model minority" yet also deemed "too passive," meaning she must work twice as hard for half the recognition.

During one meeting, Priya's male colleague received credit for her analysis, leaving her shaking with frustration. She decided to join my ERF finance seminar, a group that aims to unpack bias in the workplace. There, she shared her story about how cultural expectations often clashed with workplace demands. I guided her through a mindset reframe using the ERF framework, addressing the double bind she faced and practicing advocacy.

Priya participated in a role-play, stating, "My analysis is strategic, let's discuss it." In our diverse group, which included Black, white, and Latino colleagues, many shared similar experiences, creating a sense of solidarity. Her breakthrough came when she began using daily affirmations like, "My insights matter," which helped ease her anxiety. Additionally, she started coaching Asian women in her firm to assert their ideas.

In practice, Priya used the ERF approach to initiate meetings with "voice rounds," ensuring that marginalized voices were amplified. As a result, her promotions came swiftly, and Priya has since dedicated herself to mentoring women of color in finance, transforming her struggle into a source of inspiration for others.

ERF Practical Application Solutions:

- **Identity Power Map:** Create a visual representation of your cultural strengths, such as "Strategic thinking from my heritage." Utilize Black Feminist Theory to highlight the intersectional power of Black women, transforming anxiety into confident contributions within finance roles.

- **Emotional Anchor Exercise:** Spend three minutes focusing on your breath with the affirmation, "I release what doesn't serve me." Apply Trauma-Informed Care Theory principles to cultivate safe inner spaces, helping Black women alleviate mental fatigue and reclaim their right to thrive.

- **Growth Goal Chain:** Connect weekly actions, like "Share one idea in meetings." Leverage Academic Resilience Theory to nurture ambition, empowering Black women to transform fear into enduring career legacies.

Jada's High School Hurdle (High School)

Jada faced gender bias from male administrators who questioned her authority, resulting in emotional exhaustion, headaches, and a reluctance to advocate for Black students, which silenced her voice.

Jada is a 38-year-old Black history teacher at an urban high school in Baltimore. Growing up, she was passionate about education to escape poverty. However, in her role, she faced significant challenges. Male administrators often dismissed her curriculum ideas as "too radical" and labeled her "pushy" for advocating for Black history lessons. Coupled with the effects of racism, Jada frequently felt tokenized in her position. The emotional toll was evident. She often felt exhausted from holding back her true feelings, experienced headaches after meetings, and felt reluctant to advocate for her Black students, who needed her voice the most. As a Black woman, Jada carried the burden of having to prove herself daily, and her ambition was often dimmed by the fear of backlash.

One day, after an administrator overrode her lesson on civil rights, Jada left in tears, questioning her place in the school. She subsequently attended an ERF workshop; a space designed for teachers to discuss biases. There, she shared her story about how the childhood expectation to "be the good girl" clashed with her experiences of professional discrimination.

During the workshop, I guided her through an ERF reflection, helping her recognize the double bind she faced while using advocacy techniques. Jada practiced role-playing, stating, "My curriculum empowers students; let's collaborate." Teachers from various backgrounds shared their own struggles, creating a sense of unity among the group. Her breakthrough came when she began integrating ERF principles into daily journaling and adopted the mantra, "My voice is my power."

This practice eased her headaches and led to the formation of a student club focused on Black women's history. The teens became more open about their biases, and Jada's advocacy resulted in school-wide changes. What had once been a hurdle for her transformed into a platform for inspiring her colleagues and students to speak up.

ERF Practical Application Solutions:

- **Voice Legacy Affirmation**: Repeat the phrase, "My words build legacies." This affirmation is rooted in Black Feminist Theory and celebrates the power of Black women. It helps shift emotional exhaustion into bold classroom advocacy.

- **Boundary Healing Pause**: Take five-minute "pause breaks" to reframe biased thoughts (for example, remind yourself, "This is systemic, not me"). Drawing on Trauma-Informed Care Theory, these breaks can alleviate headaches and restore energy, honoring Black women's inherent right to healing.

- **Advocacy Ally Ladder**: Create a "ladder" of allies for support by sharing one challenge each week. This strategy is based on Academic Resilience Theory and aims to foster determination and empower Black women to transform reluctance into leadership legacies.

Elena's Salon Struggle (Hair Salon)

Elena code-switched to fit in with her clients, concealing her accent. This led to burnout, shoulder tension, and low self-worth, causing her to question her business.

Elena is a 29-year-old Dominican hairstylist in Miami's vibrant neighborhood who has brought her family's salon tradition to life. However, she often struggles with the double bind of cultural bias and gender expectations, which has taken a toll on her well-being. Most of her clients are affluent and expect her to speak with an "American" accent, forcing her to code-switch. This means softening her natural lilt and hiding her heritage to avoid losing business. The result is burnout from constantly masking her true self, along with shoulder tension that builds during her shifts and low self-worth whispering that she isn't "professional enough."

As a Latina woman, Elena faces stereotypes, such as being seen as "too loud," which makes her ambition feel like a risk. One client even commented on her "cute accent," leaving her to smile through the hurt while her shoulders tightened with tension.

Elena attended an ERF community session; a group designed for professionals facing similar challenges. There, she shared her story about how the pressures of being an immigrant clashed with the demands of salon work. During the session, I guided an exercise to help participants address the double bind and practice authenticity. Elena role-played a scenario, stating, "My heritage is my gift; let's celebrate it." The diverse group shared their own experiences, fostering connection and understanding.

Elena's breakthrough came when she began using daily affirmations, such as "My voice is my strength," which helped ease her tension. She began sharing her stories while cutting hair, and one Black client "connected with her" about facing similar biases. This transformed appointments into empowerment discussions.

As a result, Elena's salon became a sanctuary for both her and her clients. Her business flourished with a loyal clientele, and her legacy now centers around fostering cultural pride in every style she creates.

ERF Practical Application Solutions:

- **Cultural Pride Mirror:** Stand before a mirror daily, affirming "My heritage is my crown," using Black Feminist Theory to honor Black women's intersectional truth, shifting low self-worth to confident business ownership.
- **Tension Release Ritual:** Use a 5-minute shoulder roll with breaths, applying Trauma-Informed Care Theory to create safe body awareness, helping Black women release burnout as a path to thriving legacies.
- **Network Resilience Web:** Weave a "web" of 3 clients/allies for feedback (e.g., "Share one strength weekly"), drawing on Academic Resilience Theory to build ambition, empowering Black women to turn code-switching into authentic success.

Research-Based Insight: The Proven Weight of Intersectionality

Intersectionality operates as a lattice of overlapping social pressures that uniquely shape Black women's experiences. The ERF synthesizes insights from my capstone's SLR, CP, and PAP, showing how systemic racism and sexism manifest as microaggressions, bias, and subtle exclusion, creating emotional and professional strain (Gillum, 2019; Hill Collins, 2000; Moorosi et al., 2018). The SLR's analysis of 20 studies shows these experiences intensify mental health disparities, with racial discrimination amplifying childhood trauma's effects on psychological well-being and relational dynamics (Erving et al., 2021; Hamilton-Mason et al., 2009). The CP's ERF framework, drawing on Black Feminist Theory, validates these socio-cultural narratives, emphasizing how overachievement becomes a coping mechanism for Black women in professional spaces (Bertaux & Anderson, 2001; Chance, 2022). The PAP's workshop design highlights the need for culturally competent interventions to address the double bind, reducing burnout through mentorship and allyship (Luthar et al., 2000; SAMHSA, 2014). Across professions, bias shapes ambition, but for Black women, cultural and systemic pressures—like institutional racism—compound the toll, as noted in the capstone's conclusion calling for policy reforms to dismantle barriers (Hooks, 1981; Moorosi et al., 2018). The ERF offers a proven path to resilience, fostering equity by turning vulnerability into collective power, as evidenced by the capstone's emphasis on longitudinal studies to refine strategies for Black women's empowerment (Hauff et al., 2017; Xu, 2024).

Practical Strategies: Owning Your Power

From my capstone's PAP workshop, "Empower, Educate, Elevate," these strategies are for professionals in any field to dismantle the double bind:

1. **Call Out the Bind**: Say, "Bias is systemic, not personal; let's name it." I use this in corporate trainings to spark clarity.
2. **Counter Microaggressions**: Practice scripts like, "My expertise drives this discussion." I role-play these with educators.
3. **Ease Code-Switching:** Find authentic spaces, it could be lunch with allies or solo time. I guide this in therapy.

4. **Affirm Worth:** Use, "My brilliance is undeniable," especially for Black women. I share this in veteran groups.
5. **Build Allyship:** Encourage colleagues to amplify marginalized voices, a tactic I teach in higher ed.
6. **Daily Reframe:** Journal one bias encounter and reframe it as fuel for growth. From my SLR, this counters the capstone's noted mental health disparities.

Reclaiming Your Light

Every time you encounter bias, you have a choice: dim your light or shine brighter. I advise my clients, executives, teachers, and health care providers to choose one moment this week to stand tall. Speak up, claim your space, and observe how it changes the atmosphere. From the CP, the ERF's intersectional perspective demonstrates that reclaiming your light doesn't just break cycles; it transforms the double bind into a legacy of empowerment for Black women and everyone around them.

Activity Exercises: Igniting Your Fire

1. **Bias Mapping:** Identify three biases you've encountered and describe your coping strategies for each. Choose one to elevate to bold advocacy.
2. **Self-Advocacy Scripts:** Write a response to a microaggression and practice it out loud.
3. **Authenticity Check-In:** Journal about your experiences with code-switching and reflect on the spaces where you feel free to be your authentic self.
4. **Allyship Action:** Write down one way you can help amplify a colleague's voice.

Reflection Prompts:

1. When have you experienced a double bind, and how did you respond?

2. What is one microaggression you can address this week?

3. How does code-switching affect your energy, and in what situations can it be authentic?

4. What aspect of your identity can you celebrate today?

5. How can you support someone else who is facing bias?

6. Can you recall a moment when you dimmed your light? How can you reclaim that?

7. How does your role influence how you address bias?

8. What is one bold action you can take to break the cycle?

Final Reflection Question: How can you use your voice to support someone else facing a double bind today?

CHAPTER 3: Education as a Lifeline

"Education isn't a ladder—it's your wings to soar beyond limits and claim your freedom." – Dr. Lila Elliott

A 19-year-old patient stands outside, chain-smoking and without a General Educational Development (GED), declaring, "College is for people with passports." I took out my ERF mini board, which has a motivational list of optional wings. I remember being in a similar situation at 13, using a foster home couch as my desk. Twenty minutes later, he is using the facility's tablet to search for community college applications. I believe in "wings, not rungs." Let's soar with Dr. Lila Elliott and her practical ERF skills.

Flying Free Through Learning

Education didn't just save me; it became my weapon against a world built to dismiss me. As a Black woman growing up in a neighborhood where trauma was a constant presence, family instability, and the weight of systemic racism whispered that I wasn't enough, school became my sanctuary and my act of rebellion against a world that tried to confine me. Even as teachers doubted my potential, I stayed up nights scribbling notes, proving them wrong.

The hunger for learning carried me through my educational journey at Norfolk State University (NSU), Liberty University (LU), George Mason University (GMU), and concluded with my doctoral completion at UK, where I witnessed the healing power of education. Whether you are a Black woman in corporate America striving to break glass ceilings, a teacher in a high school classroom inspiring students against the odds, a therapist in a VA session guiding veterans through trauma, or a hairstylist in a salon learning to empower clients, education is your lifeline. It is the force that shatters ceilings and gives you wings to claim your freedom. For Black women, pursuing education is a fierce act of defiance against systemic barriers, but its transformative power benefits everyone.

This chapter, supported by the ERF, illustrates how learning transforms lives despite internal doubts and external gatekeepers, drawing from my 19 years of experience in teaching and healing. Let's soar together, break barriers, and build legacies that demand recognition.

Rising Through Learning
Keisha's Higher Ed Triumph (Higher Education)

Keisha struggled with imposter syndrome stemming from underfunded schools, which caused anxiety during lectures and a reluctance to pursue tenure, ultimately diminishing her ambition as a Black woman in academia.

Keisha is a 36-year-old Black adjunct professor at a college in Kentucky. She grew up in a low-income neighborhood where schools lacked books, which left her battling deep imposter syndrome that whispered "You don't belong" during her lectures. Each morning, she would start her day with sweaty palms, her voice trembling as she faced skeptical colleagues who questioned her credentials, often assuming her presence was merely filling a diversity quota.

As a Black woman in higher education, she felt the weight of systemic barriers, underfunded resources, and biased peers. This environment amplified her anxiety into heart palpitations and made her hesitant to pursue tenure for fear of rejection. The internal doubt she faced clashed with her ambition to lead, stalling her dreams.

One day, a student's comment about her "urban" accent struck a deep chord, and Keisha began to doubt her path. Seeking support, she joined my ERF university seminar, which provided a space for educators to reclaim their power.

In the seminar, she shared her story about how education had been her escape from poverty, yet the bias she faced turned it into a constant struggle. I guided the group through a goal-setting exercise using the ERF, helping participants reframe their barriers as fuel, grounded in Academic Resilience Theory. The diverse group of faculty members, including Latino and white colleagues, shared their experiences, creating a sense of solidarity.

Keisha's breakthrough came when she decided to form weekly study groups for Black students. In these groups, she shared her journey and inspired students to "unite" about their own doubts. As her anxiety eased, she gained the confidence to pursue tenure with bold proposals, ultimately earning it and establishing a resilience program. Keisha's triumph transformed her classroom into a launchpad for success, empowering future Black scholars through her legacy.

ERF Practical Application Solutions:

- **Wingspan Affirmation Flight:** Fly through daily affirmations like "My wings carry my legacy," rooted in Black Feminist Theory to affirm Black women's power, shifting imposter syndrome to confident teaching in higher ed.
- **Barrier Breath Break:** Take 5-minute breaths to release anxiety (e.g., "Inhale strength, exhale doubt"), using Trauma-Informed Care Theory to create safe pauses, helping Black women soar beyond hesitation as their birthright.
- **Mentor Resilience Chain:** Chain 3 mentors for weekly check-ins (e.g., "Share one win"), drawing on Academic Resilience Theory to build ambition, empowering Black women to turn barriers into tenure legacies.

Liam's Corporate Climb (Corporate America)

Liam felt trapped after being laid off, with self-doubt causing sleepless nights and leading to avoided training, which limited his growth and leadership potential.

Liam is a 45-year-old white sales manager living in Boston. He comes from a working-class family and recently lost his job due to downsizing. This event triggered self-doubt, reminding him of his father's experience with factory layoffs. Liam found himself tossing and turning at night under a dim bedroom light, avoiding training sessions out of fear of failure, which held him back from advancing to the Vice President position. His internal fears stalled his ambition and affected team morale, leaving him feeling disconnected from his diverse staff. As a white man, he felt the pressure to "have it together," which only intensified his hesitation.

During a meeting, his boss pointed out his avoidance behaviors, prompting Liam to realize he was stuck in his progress. He then attended an ERF corporate workshop designed to help professionals build resilience. There, he shared his story and the impact that the layoff had on his psyche. I guided him through a reframing using the ERF approach, during which we identified his doubts and set small, achievable goals grounded in Academic Resilience Theory. The diverse group, comprised of Black and Asian colleagues, also shared their own struggles, fostering a sense of connection.

Liam's breakthrough came when he decided to enroll in online leadership courses and implemented daily check-ins to track his progress. As he began mentoring his team on skill development, his sleepless nights gradually lessened. He ultimately advanced to the Vice President position and fostered a culture of learning within his organization. Liam's journey became a legacy of growth for both him and his team.

ERF Practical Application Solutions:

- **Legacy Light Affirmation:** Affirm "My path lights the way," using Black Feminist Theory to celebrate Black women's intersectional journey, shifting self-doubt to ambitious leadership in corporate roles.
- **Safe Sleep Ritual:** End days with a 5-minute reflection on wins, applying Trauma-Informed Care Theory to release sleepless nights, helping Black women claim rest as their birthright to thriving.
- **Growth Ally Ladder:** Climb with allies for goal shares (e.g., "Weekly progress call"), drawing on Academic Resilience Theory to build determination, empowering Black women to turn layoff fears into Vice President legacies.

Sofia's Therapy Growth (Private Practice)

Sofia experienced self-doubt due to family struggles, which manifested as emotional fatigue during sessions. This was compounded by cultural pressure to succeed, leading to increased burnout.

Sofia is a 31-year-old Mexican American therapist living in San Diego. Coming from an immigrant family, she grew up under the pressure to "make it," despite her parents' financial struggles. This background left her with self-doubt, which manifested as emotional fatigue during client sessions. Her long days were filled with the exhaustion of overworking to prove herself, all while fearing failure as a Latina in a predominantly white field.

Cultural expectations amplified her burnout, hindering her ability to connect with Latinx clients who needed her support. In one session, a client's story reflected the hardships of Sofia's own family, leaving her feeling overwhelmed and drained. Seeking help, she joined my ERF therapy supervision, a space designed for healers to reclaim their power. There, she "unveiled" about her experiences, the clash between immigrant dreams and her personal doubts. I guided her through a cultural affirmation exercise utilizing the ERF, incorporating Black Feminist Theory to help affirm her identity. The diverse group of therapists shared their own challenges, fostering a sense of solidarity. Sofia's breakthrough came when she decided to pursue trauma certification and began engaging in weekly cultural rituals, such as journaling in Spanish, which helped ease her fatigue. Now, she confidently supports her Latinx clients, transforming her practice into a space of empowerment. Sofia's growth has become a legacy of healing for both her and her community.

ERF Practical Application Solutions:

- **Cultural Crown Affirmation**: Crown yourself with "My roots are my crown," rooted in Black Feminist Theory to honor Black women's power, shifting fatigue to vibrant therapy leadership.
- **Energy Anchor Break:** Anchor with 5-minute pauses to reframe pressure, using Trauma-Informed Care Theory to build safe routines, helping Black women release burnout as their birthright.
- **Mentor Power Chain:** Chain mentors for skill shares (e.g., "Monthly certification check"), drawing on Academic Resilience Theory to foster ambition, empowering Black women to turn doubt into certified legacies.

Ravi's Veteran Victory (Veterans Affairs)

Ravi overcame traumatic brain injury (TBI) with the help of an ERF, but he continued to struggle with a fear of failure stemming from his combat experiences. This fear hindered his reintegration into civilian life and created mental barriers, such as isolation.

At 50, Ravi is an Asian American veteran living in Texas. He comes from a military family and returned from deployment plagued by TBI-related nightmares and a profound fear of not measuring up. This fear led him to avoid job training, further isolating him. His days were spent in his quiet home, haunted by images of combat, which strained his relationship with his wife, who struggled to understand his withdrawal. The trauma Ravi experienced stalled his ability to reintegrate, particularly as an Asian American man facing cultural pressures related to honor and vulnerability. One day, while attending a group session, a fellow veteran's story resonated deeply with him, bringing his own struggles to the surface. He decided to attend an ERF session designed for veterans to build resilience.

During this session, Ravi shared his story, revealing the horrors of combat and the weight of family expectations. I guided him through a goal-mapping exercise using the ERF, where we named his fears and applied Academic Resilience Theory to identify sources of support. The diverse group of veterans, including Black, white, and Latino individuals, shared their own pains, fostering a sense of brotherhood.

Ravi's breakthrough came when he enrolled in vocational rehabilitation (Voc Rehab) programs and began keeping daily "win logs" to reframe his understanding of failure, which helped reduce his isolation. He eventually became a mentor for younger veterans in job skills, landing a role in logistics and transforming his victory into a legacy of support. Ravi's story illustrates how education can serve as a vital lifeline for those in need.

ERF Practical Application Solutions:

- **Honor Legacy Affirmation:** Affirm "My honor builds my legacy," using Black Feminist Theory to celebrate Black women's intersectional resilience, shifting fear to confident reintegration in VA settings.
- **Isolation Release Ritual:** Release with 5-minute "connection calls" to family, applying Trauma-Informed Care Theory to create safe bonds, helping Black women heal from isolation as their birthright.
- **Support Resilience Web:** Web supports with 3 weekly touches (e.g., "Vet buddy check"), drawing on Academic Resilience Theory to build grit, empowering Black women to turn mental barriers into veteran legacies.

Research-Based Insight: The Proven Power of Education

Education functions both as a tool of liberation and a terrain of struggle for Black women. The ERF, as a proven framework from my capstone's SLR, CP, and PAP, positions education as a dual force: a tool for liberation and a battleground where systemic barriers like underfunded schools and racial discrimination intersect with internal hurdles like imposter syndrome, especially for Black women (Hamilton-Mason et al., 2009; Moorosi et al., 2018; O'Shea & Stone, 2014). The SLR's synthesis of 20 studies reveals how childhood trauma, including familial instability, community violence, impacts academic aspirations, with racial discrimination intensifying mental health disparities like depression and anxiety (Bertaux & Anderson, 2001; Erving et al., 2021). The CP highlights education as a resistance mechanism against oppression, with Black women often outperforming peers despite socioeconomic challenges, though this drive can lead to burnout (Hill Collins, 2000; Luthar et al., 2000). The PAP's workshop "Empower,

Educate, Elevate" underscores the transformative potential of culturally sensitive, trauma-informed interventions, showing how mentorship and community networks foster resilience (Hauff et al., 2017; SAMHSA, 2014). The capstone's conclusion calls for longitudinal studies to explore intersectional factors, while the introduction notes education's role in breaking intergenerational trauma cycles, supported by evidence of higher attainment despite odds (Hooks, 1981; Xu, 2024). The ERF leverages these insights, empowering Black women, with practical applications for all professionals to harness learning as a lifeline.

Practical Strategies: Seizing Education's Power

From my capstone's PAP and 19 years in education and therapy, these strategies make education actionable across settings:

1. **Frame Learning as Freedom:** Tell teams, "Every skill is a step to your power." I use this in speaking engagements to inspire Black women.
2. **Tackle Barriers:** List obstacles (e.g., access) and solutions (e.g., online courses, scholarships). I guide clients through this in VA sessions.
3. **Crush Doubts**: Affirm, "I belong in every learning space." I share this with all my students and even mentors.
4. **Set Micro-Goals:** Track small wins, like a workshop. I do this in therapy for clients.
5. **Build Networks:** Connect to learning communities, a tactic I use when I speak at international conferences.
6. **Cultural Reframe:** Journal one learning win tied to your identity weekly, from the CP's cultural competence focus.
7. **Mentor Mapping:** Pair with a mentor for monthly goals, per the PAP's mentorship emphasis.

Your Learning Spark

Education isn't limited to formal settings; it encompasses every moment of personal growth. I advise my clients to choose one thing to learn each week, even if it's just a podcast. The capstone's SLR indicates that early trauma can lead to overachievement, but the PAP demonstrates that small learning experiences, such as trainings and/or workshops, can help build resilience. That spark of learning fuels your legacy; embrace it today.

Activity Exercises: Fueling Your Flight

1. **Vision Statement:** Write how learning empowers you, with one bold goal.
2. **Barrier Buster:** List a learning goal, three barriers, and three solutions.
3. **Resilience Map:** Note one learning win and how it felt.
4. **Community Link:** List three learning resources (e.g., mentors).

Reflection Prompts:

1. How has learning changed your perception of yourself?
2. What barrier is hindering your growth, and how can you overcome it?
3. When have you doubted your place in learning, and how can you reframe that experience?
4. What is one skill you want to master, and why?
5. How can you inspire someone else to embrace learning?
6. What learning moment felt liberating to you?
7. How does your identity influence your learning journey?
8. What is one bold step you can take in your learning this week?

Final Reflection Question: What is one learning step you can take this week to empower your community?

CHAPTER 4: Theories that Heal

"Theories aren't distant dreams—they're your bold blueprint for healing and rising together." – Dr. Lila Elliott

An anxious patient sits before me, their eyes glassy. I pull out three markers: hot pink, lime green, and blue. Trauma-Informed Care Theory reminds us to breathe; Black Feminist Theory emphasizes the importance of breathing and acknowledging the racism that contributes to our trauma. One white patient dismisses it, grunting that it's just fluff. I recall a 2022 Zoom video clip on my phone, where my face went blank when a colleague suggested that my trauma research was too personal.

In the Zoom virtual room, stills capture the moment. The patient grabs the lime green marker and says, "I freeze when cops look at me like I'm a threat." Suddenly, the theory transforms into bold whiteboard graffiti, no longer distant. It becomes vivid and personal, marked by Dr. Lila Elliott's practical skills in creating art through these experiences.

Healing with Heart and Truth

When I started my doctoral journey at UK, I wasn't just pursuing a degree, I was claiming my healing. As a Black woman shaped by trauma, I carried the fight for every sister whose strength lit my path. I spent nights wrestling with doubt, surrounded by bubble-gum wrappers and research notes, fueled by the pain of childhood instability and the fire of education as my escape. Black Feminist Theory, Trauma-Informed Care Theory, and Academic Resilience Theory became my anchors, tools I wielded in therapy rooms, classrooms, and VA groups.

This chapter translates those theories into actionable strategies using the ERF. Whether you're a therapist, a professor, a corporate leader, or a barber, it proves why culturally grounded approaches aren't optional; they're essential. Theory becomes practice, practice becomes power, and power becomes a movement that lifts every professional.

Healing in Action
Nia's Social Work Sanctuary (Social Worker)

Nia felt disconnected from clients whose stories reflected her own trauma from community violence, leading to emotional exhaustion and compassion fatigue. She began to doubt her role as a Black woman in social work.

At 34, Nia was a caseworker in Philadelphia, having grown up in a tight knit but troubled neighborhood. Her childhood was marked by community violence: gunshots at night and friends lost to the streets, leaving her with a sense of hypervigilance that drained her in her social work role. The clients' stories of abuse often mirrored her experiences, resulting in emotional exhaustion. She frequently found herself in tears after shifts, questioning her impact and fearing that she couldn't "save" everyone.

As a Black woman, Nia also felt the pressure to be the "strong one," causing her to hide her pain and avoid seeking help. This only intensified her compassion fatigue. One case involved a young Black girl from a similar background, which affected Nia deeply and made her question her calling.

To address her struggles, Nia attended my ERF training, a healing space for social workers. There, she "uncovered" about her past; the gunshots she heard as a child and how they affected her physically and emotionally. I facilitated a cultural affirmation using the ERF model, grounding our discussions in Black Feminist Theory to honor her identity.

The group, consisting of diverse caseworkers, shared their own pain, fostering a sense of solidarity. Nia's breakthrough came when she decided to start affinity groups for Black families, using storytelling as a tool to build trust. In her practice, she introduced weekly "pride pauses" to affirm her own strength, helping her to mitigate feelings of exhaustion. This newfound sanctuary became a legacy for her, empowering both clients and colleagues.

ERF Practical Application Solutions:

- **Identity Healing Circle:** Circle with 2-3 peers to affirm "My Black womanhood is my sanctuary," using Black Feminist Theory to reclaim power, shifting exhaustion to connected social work for Black women.
- **Compassion Anchor Breath:** Anchor with breaths focusing on "I release what isn't mine," applying Trauma-Informed Care Theory to prevent fatigue, helping Black women claim their birthright to balanced healing.
- **Impact Goal Thread:** Thread goals with clients (e.g., "Weekly progress share"), drawing on Academic Resilience Theory to build determination, empowering Black women to turn doubt into impactful legacies.

Emma's Higher Ed Harmony (Higher Education)

Emma observed an increase in student trauma but struggled with her own unaddressed feelings of neglect, which caused hesitation in her leadership and an emotional drain in her role.

Emma is a 42-year-old white dean at a university in Ohio who comes from a rural background. Growing up with emotionally distant parents left her feeling neglected, which resulted in a fear of vulnerability that made her role in leading her department overwhelming. As student trauma, such as depression stemming from family issues and biased complaints, increased, Emma found herself hesitant to address these issues. Her own pain led to emotional exhaustion and an avoidance of deep discussions with faculty. Though she recognized her privilege as a white woman in higher education, Emma felt disconnected and questioned her ability to support a diverse student body. One meeting became particularly challenging when a Black student presented a biased complaint that overwhelmed her, stirring doubts within herself.

To find support, Emma joined an ERF retreat, a space designed for educators to heal. There, she shared her story about the lonely nights of her childhood and how they made her avoid conflict. I facilitated a safe space exercise utilizing the ERF, incorporating Trauma-Informed Care Theory principles. The diverse group of faculties shared their own struggles, fostering a sense of harmony among them.

Emma's breakthrough came when she decided to implement campus check-ins, which encouraged students to "reveal" about their feelings. In her daily practice, she now utilizes reflections to affirm her own strength, transforming her department into a supportive community. Ultimately, Emma's commitment to creating harmony has become a legacy of inclusive leadership.

ERF Practical Application Solutions:

- **Vulnerability Pride Affirm:** Affirm "My vulnerability is my strength," using Black Feminist Theory to honor Black women's power, shifting hesitation to bold higher ed leadership.
- **Drain Release Ritual:** Release with 5-minute "energy sweeps," applying Trauma-Informed Care Theory to

recharge, helping Black women claim their birthright to emotional balance.

- **Leadership Resilience Chain:** Chain faculty for goal shares (e.g., "Monthly support call"), drawing on Academic Resilience Theory to build grit, empowering Black women to turn drain into harmonious legacies.

Montez's Finance Focus (Finance)

Montez faced challenges with team morale during high-pressure situations, and his cultural fortitude masked his burnout, which ultimately affected his leadership abilities.

At 45 years old, Montez is a black banker in Virginia Beach, raised in an immigrant family with a mindset of "work hard, no complaints." However, in the high-stakes world of finance, this calm attitude concealed his burnout, stemming from long hours, team conflicts, and mental fog caused by suppressed stress. The clash between cultural expectations and leadership demands led him to overlook morale issues, which resulted in high turnover within his team. As a black male, he contended with stereotypes like being perceived as "a tech guy, not a leader," which only increased his self-doubt.

One team meeting escalated with complaints, and Montez found himself at a loss for words. He then participated in my ERF training, a supportive environment designed to help finance professionals heal. There, he "shared" how family expectations shaped his tendency to stay silent. I facilitated a goal-setting exercise that utilized the ERF and drew on Academic Resilience Theory. This diverse group of bankers shared their struggles, fostering a sense of connection and focus.

Montez's significant breakthrough came from initiating monthly goal-setting sessions, during which a story from a Latina colleague strengthened team bonds. In practice, he began using daily "focus affirmations" to combat stress, enhancing productivity. Ultimately, Montez's commitment led to the creation of resilient teams and a legacy.

ERF Practical Application Solutions:

- **Cultural Focus Affirm:** Affirm "My culture fuels my focus," using Black Feminist Theory to celebrate Black women's power, shifting burnout to sharp finance leadership.
- **Pressure Pause Anchor:** Pause with breaths to "anchor in calm," applying Trauma-Informed Care Theory to hide no more, helping Black women claim their birthright to stress-free thriving.
- **Morale Goal Web:** Web team for morale shares (e.g., "Weekly win circle"), drawing on Academic Resilience Theory to build grit, empowering Black women to turn pressure into legacy teams.

Tamika's Loc's Crown (Loctician)

Tamika grappled with doubts about her role as a community staple. Long shifts contributed to physical tension in her back, adding to her burdens. Additionally, as a Black woman, she often faced stereotypes, such as being labeled "just a loctician," which further eroded her sense of self-worth.

A pivotal moment occurred when a young Black girl, one of her clients, shared her own grief, causing Tamika's pain to resurface and leaving her momentarily frozen. Seeking support, she attended an ERF talk designed for everyday professionals, where she "exposed" how loss had stolen her crown.

In this safe space, guided by a focus on cultural reflection and Black Feminist Theory, Tamika and a diverse group of stylists shared their own experiences of pain, which rekindled her passion. Her breakthrough came through heart-to-heart conversations during loc styles, where she helped a biracial client process grief. To reinforce her resilience, Tamika began keeping a nightly journal that affirmed her strength and focused on turning her salon into a hub for community healing. Ultimately, her journey transformed her pain into a legacy of resilience for her community.

ERF Practical Application Solutions:

- **Crown Legacy Affirm:** Affirm "My crown lights," using Black Feminist Theory to honor Black women's power, shifting numbness to passionate business leadership.
- **Loss Release Ritual:** Release with 5-minute "crown breaths," applying Trauma-Informed Care Theory to heal isolation, helping Black women claim their birthright to emotional crown.
- **Community Resilience Chain:** Chain clients for shares (e.g., "Weekly story swap"), drawing on Academic Resilience Theory to build grit, empowering Black women to turn pain into some crown legacies.

Research-Based Insight: The Proven Power of Healing Theories

The ERF translates theory into practice, combining Black Feminist Theory, Trauma-Informed Care Theory, and Academic Resilience Theory to create a cohesive approach to healing. Black Feminist Theory centers the intersectional realities of Black women, validating their resilience against oppression, a showing cultural narrative as key to overcoming trauma (Moorosi et al., 2018). Trauma-Informed Care Theory, per SAMHSA (2014), addresses trauma's universal impact— emotional regulation issues, physical symptoms— compounded for Black women by systemic stressors like racism, as noted in the CP and PAP (Gillum, 2019; Hauff et al., 2017). Academic Resilience Theory, per Martin and Marsh

(2006), highlights protective factors like community support, critical for Black women's academic drive despite burnout risks, as the SLR and PAP emphasize (Luthar et al., 2000; O'Shea & Stone, 2014). The capstone's introduction and conclusion call for culturally sensitive interventions, with the PAP's workshop "Empower, Educate, Elevate" proving that mentorship enhances outcomes (Hooks, 1981; Xu, 2024). The ERF synthesizes these, offering a holistic approach to heal Black women and all professionals, turning theories into actionable legacies (Bertaux & Anderson, 2001; Chance, 2022).

Practical Strategies: Making Theories Real

From my capstone's PAP and 19 years of practice, these strategies bring theories to life:

1. **Center Identity:** Affirm diverse voices in meetings, as I do in workshops, using Black Feminist Theory.
2. **Create Safety:** Use trauma-informed check-ins (e.g., "How's your energy today?"), a staple in my therapy.
3. **Foster Resilience:** Set goals with mentors, per my trainings, using Academic Resilience Theory.
4. **Blend Cultural Tools:** Use storytelling or cultural rituals, as I guide with clients, from the CP's focus.
5. **Integrate Daily:** Combine approaches in work, e.g., daily reflections, as the PAP suggests.
6. **Build Community:** Host "theory shares" monthly, from the capstone's community emphasis.
7. **Evaluate Impact:** Track one healing action weekly, aligning with the capstone's call for longitudinal study.

Your Healing Blueprint

Choose one approach today: affirm a colleague's identity, create a safe moment, or set a goal. I remind my clients that small steps lead to significant healing. From the capstone's SLR, we see that trauma can lead to overachievement, while the PAP indicates that trainings and/or workshops like mine foster resilience. Your journey begins now, so take the opportunity to shape your legacy.

Activity Exercises: Activating Healing

1. **Theory in Action:** Apply one theory to your life with a 10-minute plan.
2. **Empowerment Quotes:** Write three quotes, one per theory, to inspire.
3. **Resilience Plan:** Note one goal tied to a theory.
4. **Cultural Connection:** List one cultural strength you can use.

Reflection Prompts:

1. Which theory resonates with you the most, and why?
2. How can you create a safe space for someone today?
3. What is one strength that your identity contributes to the healing process?
4. How has trauma influenced your professional approach?
5. What is one way you can apply a theory in your work?
6. When did you feel most empowered, and how can you recreate that experience?
7. How can you support a colleague in their healing journey?
8. What's one bold healing step you can take?

Final Reflection Question: How can you incorporate these theories into your professional interactions to inspire and uplift others?

CHAPTER 5: Building the Framework

"Build the framework of your dreams—sturdy, bold, and ready to hold legacies untold." – Dr. Lila Elliott

At 3:45 a.m., a suicide call ends at the VA 988 line. My colleague, Mr. Lex, a white male, slams the file down on the desk and exclaims, "These cases break me." I grab three Lego bricks labeled "dignity," "pride," and "self-determination" and place them on the desk. "Now, stack yours, Mr. Lex." He starts shaky, but by 4:05, his tower proudly displays the name of Shon, the caller he just saved. This framework is built on countless burnt coffee breaks and practical skills learned from Dr. Lila Elliott and the ERF. Together, we're building resilience, piece by piece.

Your Blueprint for Change

At UK, it was not just about earning a degree; it was about creating a bridge from my pain to my purpose as a Black woman who has survived trauma. I remember those late nights and papers scattered across my lap with my MacBook warm from being on for hours, wrestling with doubt as I crafted the ERF, fueled by the memories of childhood instability and the transformative power of education. I have witnessed Black women reclaim their power, educators anchor themselves in community, and finance leaders take back their voices, all with measurable impact.

The ERF is that bridge, born from my doctoral research, blending dignity, pride, and self-determination into a valuable tool for every professional, whether you are a parent, a therapist guiding clients, a professor shaping young minds, a veteran rebuilding your life, or a *mentor* uplifting your community. This chapter provides a step-by-step guide to building your own ERF framework, so you can create a legacy that lasts.

Frameworks in Motion
Aisha's Therapy Build (Private Practice)

Aisha felt overwhelmed by her client load, which mirrored her feelings of neglect, self-doubt, and fatigue, hindering her impact as a Black therapist.

Aisha, 39, a Brooklyn therapist raised in foster care, built her practice to give children the stability she never had. However, the stories of abandonment from her clients echoed her own experiences, leading to self-doubt that made her therapy sessions feel forced. The fatigue left her drained after long hours of work. Every morning hit her with dread and a mind racing through crises that mirrored her own unstable childhood. The real challenge was dealing with the echo of trauma, which led her to avoid cultural discussions out of fear of burnout.

As a Black woman, Aisha faced biases, often being labeled as "the trauma expert" without adequate support, which only amplified her feelings of isolation. Long nights and empty coffee cups became routine. One client, a Black teen, triggered a deep emotional response in Aisha, causing her to feel her foundation begin to crack. Seeking help, she joined my ERF session, a safe space for healers. There, she "denuded" about her story, sharing the instability of her foster home experiences and how they lingered within her. I guided her through a dignity exercise using the ERF method, which affirmed her cultural pride with proverbs from her heritage.

The diverse group of therapists shared their own pains, creating a sense of community and support. Aisha's breakthrough came when she began co-creating therapy plans with her Black clients, incorporating cultural wisdom into her practice.

She implemented weekly "pride pauses" to recharge, transforming her practice into a legacy of healing. Aisha's journey became a beacon of hope for other Black therapists.

ERF Practical Application Solutions:

- **Dignity Legacy Affirm:** Affirm "My dignity builds my legacy," using Black Feminist Theory to honor Black women's power, shifting self-doubt to confident therapy leadership.
- **Fatigue Release Anchor:** Anchor with 5-minute "release breaths," applying Trauma-Informed Care Theory to ease drain, helping Black women claim their birthright to energized healing.
- **Impact Goal Web:** Web clients for goal shares (e.g., "Weekly progress thread"), drawing on Academic Resilience Theory to build determination, empowering Black women to turn fatigue into impactful legacies.

Mark's Corporate Construct (Corporate America)

Mark observed that his team was divided due to stress, while his unresolved trauma from job loss was hindering his leadership and impacting morale.

Mark is a 48-year-old white executive living in Charlotte, North Carolina, hailing from a blue-collar family. He experienced significant trauma after losing his father due to a factory layoff, which led him to avoid team conflicts and fear failure. In his office, there was a pervasive tension characterized by high turnover, low morale, and staff disagreements over projects, reflecting his own unaddressed pain. His hesitation to lead boldly was rooted in sleepless nights spent replaying his father's layoff, which created a disconnect between him and his diverse team.

As a white man, Mark felt a sense of privilege but remained unaware of the struggles faced by his team, which deepened his self-doubt. A particularly intense conflict among the team left him feeling overwhelmed, with papers scattered across his desk. Seeking to improve the situation, he attended my ERF Microsoft Teams Webinar, a supportive environment for executives. There, he "unwrapped" about the deep impact of the layoff on his mental health. I facilitated a self-determination exercise using the ERF, helping him identify supports such as a mentor.

During this session, the diverse group of executives shared their own struggles, fostering a sense of community. Mark's breakthrough came when he began facilitating goal-setting meetings, where contributions from a Black employee sparked the implementation of diversity initiatives.

In practice, Mark initiated daily "win shares" with his team to build unity, ultimately transforming his group into a resilient legacy. His journey evolved into a model for corporate healing, demonstrating the power of vulnerability and collaboration in leadership.

ERF Practical Application Solutions:

- **Pride Legacy Map:** Map cultural strengths for the team (e.g., "Share one pride story weekly"), using Black Feminist Theory to celebrate Black women's power, shifting division to inclusive corporate leadership.
- **Stress Safe Pause:** Pause with "stress sweeps," applying Trauma-Informed Care Theory to release hesitation, helping Black women claim their birthright to stress-free teamwork.
- **Determination Goal Chain:** Chain team actions for morale (e.g., "Weekly ally check"), drawing on Academic Resilience Theory to build grit, empowering Black women to turn stress into legacy teams.

Lila's High School Foundation (High School)

Lila struggled with burnout due to cultural pressures and emotional exhaustion, which affected her student engagement and teaching purpose.

Lila is a 33-year-old Puerto Rican teacher in Miami who comes from an immigrant family. Growing up, she felt immense pressure to "work hard," but in her high school classroom, this pressure led to burnout. She experienced emotional exhaustion from overplanning, frequent headaches from stress, and doubts about her ability to impact her students positively. Her days were often a blur of lesson plans, and her voice grew hoarse from explaining concepts to disengaged teens. The cultural expectations to succeed drained her energy. The clash between these expectations and the demands of teaching hindered her ability to engage her students.

As a Latina, Lila also faced bias, often being pigeonholed as "the diversity teacher," which added to her fatigue. She spent late nights grading and frequently skipped breaks. After one student walkout, she began to question her role, with papers scattered on her desk in disarray.

To find support, Lila joined my ERF lunch and learn, a space designed for educators to share their experiences. There, she "spoke" about her struggles as an immigrant and the pressure she felt to prove herself. I facilitated a pride exercise using the ERF, helping her recognize and celebrate her heritage through family stories.

The group, which consisted of diverse teachers, shared their own challenges, creating a strong foundation of support. Lila's breakthrough came when she started implementing student-led clubs, where kids set their own goals. In practice, she now uses daily "pride moments" to recharge, transforming her classroom into a legacy of empowerment. Lila's journey has turned her foundation into a beacon for Latinx educators.

ERF Practical Application Solutions:

- **Self-Determination Pride Affirm**: Affirm "My pride drives my determination," using Black Feminist Theory to honor Black women's power, shifting burnout to passionate teaching.
- **Drain Healing Ritual**: Heal with "energy rituals," applying Trauma-Informed Care to release drain, helping Black women claim their birthright to energized classrooms.
- **Engagement Resilience Ladder**: Ladder goals with students (e.g., "Weekly share"), drawing on Academic Resilience Theory to build grit, empowering Black women to turn doubt into legacy foundations.

Jamal's Veteran Vision (Veterans Affairs)

Jamal felt lost after his service. Isolation hindered his reintegration, and he struggled with mental barriers caused by trauma.

Jamal is a 55-year-old Black veteran from Quantico, hailing from a military family. After his deployment, he returned home with major depressive disorder and felt lost in civilian life. He isolated himself to avoid social events and struggled with mental barriers, thinking "I'm broken," which strained his family ties due to irritability. His days were quiet, and his apartment became a refuge from the crowded VA halls, but his mind was haunted by the horrors of combat.

The core issue was trauma's grip on him, which hindered his ability to pursue job training and form connections. As a Black man, he faced stereotypes like "tough guy," which made him even more reluctant to seek help. He spent late nights staring at job ads and avoiding phone calls.

During one VA group session, he sat silently, his hands clenched. He later attended my ERF group, a safe space for veterans. There, he shared his story about the traumas of combat and the strain on his family. I facilitated a mapping exercise using the ERF, where he named his fears.

The diverse group of veterans shared their own pains, which helped create a sense of vision. His breakthrough came when he engaged in job training and started using "win journals" to combat his isolation. Now, he mentors younger veterans, turning his healing into a living legacy of brotherhood and leadership. Jamal's story proves what my doctoral research found: education isn't optional; it's a lifeline.

ERF Practical Application Solutions:

- **Vision Legacy Affirm**: Affirm "My vision builds my legacy," using Black Feminist Theory to honor Black women's power, shifting isolation to connected veteran leadership.
- **Grip Release Anchor**: Anchor with "release grips," applying Trauma-Informed Care Theory to ease mental barriers, helping Black women claim their birthright to freedom from trauma.
- **Reintegration Goal Web**: Web supports for goals (e.g., "Weekly vet call"), drawing on Academic Resilience Theory to build grit, empowering Black women to turn loss into reintegration legacies.

Research-Based Insight: The ERF's Proven Strength

The ERF, as a proven framework from my doctoral research of the SLR, CP, and PAP, validates Black women's resilience against oppression (Hill Collins, 2000; Moorosi et al., 2018). The SLR's synthesis shows socioeconomic factors and family instability impede educational achievements, yet Black women often outperform peers, a resilience noted in the CP (Bertaux & Anderson, 2001; O'Shea & Stone, 2014). Trauma-Informed Care Theory, per SAMHSA (2014), addresses trauma's physical and emotional toll, compounded for Black women by racism, as the PAP's workshop "Empower, Educate, Elevate" proves with culturally sensitive support (Gillum, 2019; Hauff et al., 2017). Academic Resilience Theory, per Martin and Marsh (2006), highlights community and mentorship as buffers, reducing burnout risks identified in the capstone's conclusion (Luthar et al., 2000; Xu, 2024). The introduction emphasizes education's role in breaking cycles, while the PAP shows that the ERF's values, dignity, pride, and self-determination enhance outcomes through practical applications (Hooks, 1981; Chance, 2022). This holistic approach empowers Black women and all professionals to build sturdy legacies.

Practical Strategies: Step-by-Step Building

From my capstone's PAP and 19 years of practice, these strategies construct your framework:

1. **Start with Dignity:** Validate team experiences in check-ins, as I do in workshops.
2. **Infuse Pride:** Celebrate cultural strengths through storytelling, a CP focus.
3. **Foster Self-Determination:** Co-create goals, per my trainings.
4. **Use Case Studies:** Share success stories in team huddles, from the PAP.
5. **Integrate Daily:** Apply ERF values in reflections, aligning with capstone's call.
6. **Build Support:** Map allies weekly, a tactic from the SLR's community emphasis.
7. **Evaluate Growth:** Track one action's impact monthly, per the conclusion's research need.

Your First Brick

Lay one ERF brick today, whether it's a kind word, a personal goal, or a cultural acknowledgment. I tell my clients that every small act contributes to building their legacy. Your brick begins now; take charge of your foundation.

Activity Exercises: Constructing Your Base

1. **Framework Map:** Chart strengths, needs, supports.
2. **Daily Alignment:** Track one ERF-aligned action.
3. **Resilience Goal:** Set one goal tied to ERF values.
4. **Team Connection:** Note one way to share the ERF.

Reflection Prompts:

1. Where do you see resilience in your work?
2. How can you honor someone's dignity today?
3. What cultural pride can you bring to your role?
4. What is one goal you can set for self-determination?
5. How has the ERF inspired your leadership?
6. When did you feel most empowered, and why?
7. How can you share the ERF with your team?
8. What is one bold step you can take to build your legacy?

Final Reflection Question: How will the ERF influence your professional legacy starting today?

CHAPTER 6: The Power of Culturally Rooted Support

"Root yourself in culture's soil—watch your resilience bloom and connect us all." – Dr. Lila Elliott

At 7:30 p.m., I drag the ERF tree drawing into the group. Our Latina patient, Sandra, expresses that there is no service for her mother, who is detained by ICE. Viola, a volunteer stylist, pops in with shea butter and begins braiding Sandra's hair, ribbon by ribbon. By 8:11, the tin of ashes has a blue ribbon painted across the top, while bachata music plays from my phone. The roots of our support are buttered scalps and borrowed Wi-Fi, and we find joy in the bloom of Sandra humming as she colors her tree leaves pink. Let's support our neighbors by utilizing Dr. Lila Elliott's ERF practical skills.

Growing Strong Together

Community has been my lifeline. As a Black woman, I found strength in circles of Black women, through my grandmother's kitchen table stories and mentors who recognized my potential when I couldn't see it myself. I remember late nights surrounded by notes and the smell of scented candles, driven by the desire to create something for my sisters who face systemic barriers. Culturally rooted support through representation, safe spaces, and mentorship is not optional. It is a professional asset. Whether you're a social worker advocating for families, a professor mentoring students, a corporate leader fostering team bonds, or a psychologist uplifting clients, you need a network that fortifies you.

This chapter utilizes the ERF to help you build your resilience village, drawing from my experiences at the VA, UK, and at Riverside. Together, let's thrive and create legacies that unite us all.

Villages of Strength
Bee's Social Work Circle (Social Worker)

Bee felt alone with racial bias in her agency, exhaustion from microaggressions leading to burnout, and isolation.

Bee is a 39-year-old Black social worker in South Carolina from a community-focused family. She navigates racial bias in her child welfare agency, experiencing microaggressions such as being second-guessed on cases involving Black families.

These challenges leave her exhausted after shifts and isolated from colleagues who don't understand the cultural burdens she carries. Her days often blur into a cycle of paperwork, and her spirit is drained by comments like "You're too emotional," a stereotype she confronts daily.

This double bind intensifies her burnout, causing her to question her role as a Black woman in a system that frequently dismisses her insights. One of her memorable cases, involving the removal of a Black child, felt too personal for her. Bee broke down in her car, with tears staining her notes.

Seeking support, she joined my ERF architect lab, which is designed for social workers on Saturdays. In this space, she shared her experiences, including the community bias she grew up with and the weight it still carries. I facilitated a support circle using the ERF, focusing on cultural pride and the power of shared meals. The group, made up of diverse social workers, exchanged their pains, creating a supportive environment.

Bee's breakthrough came from initiating weekly lunches for her Black colleagues, allowing them to share their resilience stories. In her practice, she employs "pride shares" to recharge, effectively reducing burnout, and she also launched a mentorship program for Black youth. Ultimately, Bee's circle became a legacy of work office strength.

ERF Practical Application Solutions:

- **Pride Circle Affirm:** Affirm "My circle roots my pride," using Black Feminist Theory to celebrate Black women's power, shifting isolation to connected social work leadership.
- **Bias Safe Anchor:** Anchor with "safe shares," applying Trauma-Informed Care Theory to release exhaustion, helping Black women claim their birthright to bias-free healing.
- **Mentor Resilience Web:** Web colleagues for mentorship (e.g., "Weekly story swap"), drawing on Academic Resilience Theory to build grit, empowering Black women to turn bias into legacy circles.

Rani's Higher Ed Network (Higher Education)

Rani observed that South Asian students felt isolated, with cultural stigma surrounding mental health obstructing his ability to provide support and leadership.

Rani is a 40-year-old Indian American professor living in Boston, hailing from a family of educators. He observed that many South Asian students felt isolated, with their mental health struggles hidden by cultural stigma, often summarized by the phrase "don't air dirty laundry." In his quiet office, his attempts to offer support were met with silence, and he felt increasing discomfort in his role as a professor. The clash between cultural pressures and leadership demands led to distant relationships and self-doubt regarding his effectiveness.

As an Indian American, he grappled with stereotypes such as the "model minority," which heightened his hesitation to reach out. The situation became more urgent when one student dropped out, citing stress, making Rani acutely aware of the consequences of his inaction.

Seeking solutions, he attended my ERF seminar designed for educators. There, he shared his experience and the family expectations that contributed to his silence. I facilitated a network mapping exercise using the ERF framework, which focused on celebrating cultural pride through group dinners. The diverse group of professors exchanged their struggles, creating a supportive network.

Rani's breakthrough came when he initiated monthly dinners for South Asian students, where they could discuss issues of bias over homemade chai. In practice, he started using "pride talks" to foster connections, transforming his department into a supportive community. Through these efforts, Rani created a legacy of inclusion.

ERF Practical Application Solutions:

- **Network Legacy Affirm:** Affirm "My network builds my legacy," using Black Feminist Theory to honor Black women's power, shifting stigma to connected higher ed leadership.
- **Stigma Release Ritual:** Release with "stigma sweeps," applying Trauma-Informed Care Theory to ease discomfort, helping Black women claim their birthright to stigma-free support.
- **Support Goal Chain:** Chain students for goal shares (e.g., "Weekly check-in"), drawing on Academic Resilience Theory to build grit, empowering Black women to turn isolation into legacy networks.

Beth's Finance Fellowship (Finance)

Beth recognized gaps in team diversity, her discomfort with bias discussions undermining leadership and morale.

Beth is a 29-year-old biracial accountant living in Boston, originally from a small town. She noticed the diversity gaps in her finance team, where Black and Latina colleagues were often overlooked. Her discomfort with discussions about bias made her avoid addressing these issues, which weakened leadership and lowered morale within her team. The atmosphere in her office was tense, meetings felt awkward, and her attempts to promote inclusion were met with silence.

Beth's unaddressed privilege created hesitation and division among her colleagues. As a biracial woman, she felt immense pressure to "get it right," which amplified her self-doubt. She spent late nights overanalyzing emails and avoiding difficult conversations.

During a team feedback session, concerns about turnover were raised, and Beth felt lost. In response, she decided to join an ERF program tailored for finance professionals. There, she "vented" about her experiences and how her background had blinded her to issues of bias. I facilitated an ally exercise within the ERF, which encouraged bonding through shared lunches. The diverse group of accountants shared their struggles, fostering connections among them.

Beth's breakthrough came when she initiated a women's network that organized lunches for sharing experiences. Now, in her daily practice, she implements "inclusion checks" to ensure that all voices are heard, transforming her team into a model of equity. Beth's journey has become a beacon for promoting inclusivity in the finance industry.

ERF Practical Application Solutions:

- **Fellowship Pride Affirm:** Affirm "My fellowship roots pride," using Black Feminist Theory to celebrate Black women's power, shifting discomfort to inclusive finance leadership.
- **Gap Safe Pause:** Pause with "gap reflections," applying Trauma-Informed Care Theory to release

hesitation, helping Black women claim their birthright to gap-free teams.

- **Morale Resilience Ladder:** Ladder team goals (e.g., "Weekly share"), drawing on Academic Resilience Theory to build grit, empowering Black women to turn gaps into legacy fellowships.

Ana's Salon Sisterhood (Hair Salon)

Ana desired deeper connections but felt emotionally drained by client stories that mirrored her immigration trauma, which was dulling her business.

Ana is a 32-year-old Dominican stylist in New York who came from a family business. She immigrated at a young age and carried the trauma of separation anxiety with her, which emotionally drained her during conversations with clients, making her salon feel superficial. Her days were long, filled with the sound of scissors snipping through hair while clients shared their stories of loss, mirroring her own pain from leaving her siblings. This emotional burden left her feeling quiet and filled with doubt about her role as a stylist.

Ana's trauma dulled her spirit, leading to feelings of isolation and causing her to question her impact on the community. As a Latina, she faced stereotypes such as being "too emotional," which only intensified her struggle. One day, a client spoke about their grief related to immigration, and Ana felt her own trauma resurface, her hands trembling. Hoping to find solace, she attended an ERF talk, a supportive space for professionals. There, she shared her story about the family separation and her longing for connection. I guided the group through a sisterhood exercise using the ERF framework, focusing on cultural pride through music and shared stories. The diverse group of stylists' "song" about their own pains created a sense of sisterhood.

Ana's breakthrough came during story nights in her

salon, where a Black client's tale inspired group support. In her practice, she began using "pride rituals" to recharge, transforming her salon into a legacy of healing. Ana's sisterhood became a beacon of community support.

ERF Practical Application Solutions:

- **Sisterhood Legacy Affirm**: Affirm "My sisterhood builds my legacy," using Black Feminist Theory to honor Black women's power, shifting drain to vibrant salon leadership.
- **Drain Release Anchor**: Anchor with "drain releases," applying Trauma-Informed Care to ease emotional load, helping Black women claim their birthright to energized connections.
- **Connection Goal Chain**: Chain clients for shares (e.g., "Weekly story"), drawing on Academic Resilience Theory to build grit, empowering Black women to turn drain into legacy sisterhoods.

Research-Based Insight: The Proven Power of Community

The ERF, as a proven framework from my SLR, CP, and PAP, leverages culturally rooted support to counter trauma's isolation, with Black Feminist Theory emphasizing intersectional identities to resilience (Hill Collins, 2000; SAMHSA, 2014). The SLR's shows representation, and safe spaces reduce mental health disparities for Black women, compounded by systemic inequities (Gillum, 2019; Moorosi et al., 2018). The CP emphasizes mentorship and peer support as key mechanisms for sustaining academic engagement and professional persistence (Bertaux & Anderson, 2001; Martin & Marsh, 2006). PAP workshops, like "Empower, Educate, Elevate," operationalize these findings, showing that culturally informed interventions strengthen relational networks, improve coping, and reduce burnout (Hauff et al., 2017; O'Shea & Stone, 2014). The conclusion calls for longitudinal studies to refine support, while the capstone notes community's role in breaking cycles (Hooks, 1981; Xu, 2024). ERF positions relational support as an essential component for thriving, enabling Black women and professionals to navigate challenges collectively while achieving sustained growth.

Practical Strategies: Fostering Support

From my capstone's PAP and 19 years of practice, these strategies grow your village:

1. **Promote Representation:** Include diverse voices in teams, just as I do in my workshops.
2. **Create Safe Spaces:** Encourage open dialogue in meetings, focused on cultural perspectives.
3. **Encourage Mentorship:** Pair individuals with cultural allies, following the guidelines from my training sessions.
4. **Design Cultural Workshops:** Incorporate storytelling and rituals, as I guide clients through these processes.
5. **Build Networks:** Map out support systems weekly, emphasizing the community aspect of SLR.
6. **Celebrate Roots:** Organize monthly "Culture Days" that align with the project's goals.
7. **Evaluate Bonds:** Track the impact of one connection each week, based on the conclusions drawn.

Your Village Seed

Plant one connection today, a mentor, a group, or a kind word. I tell clients that your village starts with one step. From the SLR, it is understood that isolation drives trauma, but plant your seed now and watch it bloom. So, you are not alone. We are in this together!

Activity Exercises: Nurturing Roots

1. **Community Audit:** Evaluate your network and identify growth opportunities.
2. **Mentor Letter:** Compose a message to a potential mentor.
3. **Support Map:** Create a diagram of your support network.
4. **Cultural Ritual:** Plan one culturally affirming act.

Reflection Prompts:

1. Who truly understands you, and how can you connect more with them?
2. What is one way to create a safe space at work?
3. How does your culture enhance your resilience?
4. Who can you mentor this week?
5. What community need can you help address?
6. When have you felt most supported, and why?
7. How can you amplify a colleague's voice?
8. What is one bold step you can take to expand your network?

Final Reflection Question: What is one action you can take to enhance cultural support in your workplace?

CHAPTER 7: From Surviving to Thriving

"Survival is your story's start—thriving is the epic legacy you write next." – Dr. Lila Elliott

Monday: At the Department of Veterans Affairs, I managed to avert a suicidal plan despite feeling sleepless.

Tuesday: In my Criminal Justice class, 30 undergraduates referenced my ERF data, indicating they are thriving.

Wednesday: At the Riverside, a patient hugged me goodbye and said, "You taught me to fold laundry like fractions," which showed how they are thriving.

Thursday: My own panic attack story from 2023 became a case study in my Doctoral Journey; it's part of my legacy.

From grit to glory, it's the same week for the same girl who once chewed bubble gum for courage. Now, she is the author of this self-help journal: Dr. Lila Elliott.

From Grit to Glory

I've survived trauma, bias, and the challenges of being a Black woman in a world that often tries to break me. Growing up, I navigated family chaos and systemic racism, using education as my shield, even when doubt crept in during late nights spent studying for my doctoral degree at UK.

My experience taught me that surviving is just the starting point. Whether you're a Black woman in social work carrying the pain of your clients, a teacher in a high school fighting through burnout, a therapist in a VA session battling your own scars, a parent, and/or just a person concealing your own wounds, thriving is your birthright.

This chapter uses the ERF to guide you from survival to thriving through mindset changes, advocacy, and cultural healing, drawing from my doctoral call to break intergenerational cycles.

Let's write powerful stories together that redefine your legacy.

Thriving Tales
Tanya's Social Work Shift (Social Worker)

Tanya overcame burnout resulting from her own trauma and the emotional fatigue caused by overidentifying with her clients.

Tanya is a 38-year-old Black caseworker in New Orleans who is passionate about supporting youth. Growing up in poverty with a mother battling addiction kept her in survival mode, making it hard to step back from her clients' pain. This emotional connection often led to fatigue. Some nights she cried after work, questioning whether she could separate her story from theirs. Long days and a desk buried in case files left her carrying the weight of a young Black girl's relapse; a mirror of her mother's struggle. The grip of trauma amplified her burnout in such a high-stakes role. As a Black woman, she felt immense pressure to "save" Black youth without adequate support, leading to feelings of isolation. She skipped meals and kept to herself, retreating from peers as the stress mounted.

One particularly devastating incident, a client's overdose, left Tanya feeling defeated and drained. Seeking help, she attended an ERF annual refresher designed for social workers. There, she openly shared her story, discussing the impact of addiction and the guilt that accompanied it. I guided her through affirmations using the ERF approach, helping her reframe her doubts with phrases like "I am enough."
During the training, the diverse group of caseworkers shared their own pain, fostering a sense of community and healing.

Tanya's breakthrough came when she started advocating for self-care resources and eventually thrived in her role as a team leader. In her practice, she implemented daily "thrive checks" to help herself detach from the emotional burdens of her work. This transformation turned her practice into a legacy of balanced healing, making Tanya a beacon of hope for Black social workers.

ERF Practical Application Solutions:

- **Thrive Legacy Affirm:** Affirm "My thrive writes my legacy," using Black Feminist Theory to honor Black women's power, shifting fatigue to vibrant social work leadership.
- **Fatigue Healing Pause:** Heal with "pause breaks," applying Trauma-Informed Care Theory to release overidentification, easing Black women's birthright to balanced thriving.
- **Detachment Goal Chain:** Chain self-care actions (e.g., "Weekly boundary set"), drawing on Academic Resilience Theory to build grit, empowering Black women to turn burnout into thriving legacies.

Mike's Higher Ed Harmony (Higher Education)

Mike felt trapped in survival mode due to past failures, with self-doubt impacting his decisions and faculty inspiration.

Mike, a 45-year-old white administrator in Wisconsin from a working-class background, felt stuck in survival mode after past job failures. Self-doubt led to hesitation in his decisions and disengagement during faculty meetings. His office was quiet, and his mind replayed old rejections, causing his leadership to falter as staff members became increasingly disengaged. The lingering effects of trauma limited his effectiveness in higher education. As a white man, he felt pressure to "have it all together," which amplified his feelings of isolation. He spent late nights overanalyzing emails and avoiding bold decisions.

One faculty meeting fell flat, and Mike began to doubt his impact. In search of support, he joined my ERF's monthly check-in, a space designed for educators to share their experiences. During the seminar, he shared how his past failures had affected his mental well-being. I guided the group in advocating for wellness with the mantra, "Your voice matters." The diverse group of faculty members shared their own struggles, fostering a sense of harmony.

Mike's breakthrough came when he recognized the value of wellness programs, which allowed him to thrive personally and reignite his energy. In his practice, he implemented "harmony checks" to inspire his colleagues, transforming his department into a supportive legacy. Mike's focus on harmony became a guiding light for higher education leaders.

ERF Practical Application Solutions:

- **Harmony Legacy Affirm:** Affirm "My harmony builds my legacy," using Black Feminist Theory to honor Black women's power, shifting doubt to harmonious higher ed leadership.
- **Doubt Release Ritual:** Release with "doubt sweeps," applying Trauma-Informed Care Theory to ease isolation, helping Black women claim their birthright to confident harmony.
- **Inspiration Resilience Ladder:** Ladder goals for faculty (e.g., "Weekly win share"), drawing on Academic Resilience Theory to build grit, empowering Black women to turn doubt into legacy harmony.

Sophia's Therapy Transformation (Private Practice)

Sophia struggled with self-doubt due to pressures from her family and the demands of cultural success, which intensified her burnout in her role.

Sophia is a 30-year-old Indian American counselor based in Seattle, hailing from an immigrant family. She struggled with self-doubt, largely due to family pressures to "succeed." These cultural demands intensified her burnout, leading to emotional fatigue during client sessions and causing her to hesitate in trying new therapeutic techniques. Her office was cluttered with client files, and her mind was constantly racing with expectations to be the "perfect" healer, leaving her energy depleted from overworking. The pressure she felt hindered her effectiveness, particularly when working with Indian clients who needed cultural understanding. As an Indian American woman, she was also burdened by stereotypes such as being labeled an "overachiever," which added additional layers of stress.

During one session, Sophia felt stuck and inadequate, her spirit drained from the weight of expectations.

In search of support, she joined my ERF group, a safe space for healers to share their experiences. There, Sophia "bared" about her family's expectations and the cultural weight she carried.

I guided the group in incorporating cultural rituals alongside the ERF, combining theoretical insights with meditation practices. The diverse group of counselors shared their own struggles, fostering an environment of understanding and transformation. Sophia experienced a significant breakthrough; she gained confidence in guiding her clients and felt empowered to implement new techniques in her practice.

Now, she uses rituals to recharge, transforming her therapy sessions into a legacy of healing. Sophia's journey has become an inspiration for other Indian American counselors, serving as a beacon of hope and resilience.

ERF Practical Application Solutions:

- **Transformation Legacy Affirm:** Affirm "My transformation writes my legacy," using Black Feminist Theory to honor Black women's power, shifting doubt to confident therapy leadership.
- **Burnout Anchor Exercise:** Anchor with 5-minute "burnout releases," applying Trauma-Informed Care Theory to ease fatigue, helping Black women claim their birthright to transformed energy.
- **Innovation Goal Chain:** Chain innovative actions (e.g., "Weekly new tool"), drawing on Academic Resilience Theory to build grit, empowering Black women to turn pressure into legacy transformations.

Carlos's Veteran Victory (Veterans Affairs)

Carlos transitioned from surviving a suicidal attempt, where isolation hindered his reintegration and created mental barriers.

Carlos is a 52-year-old Puerto Rican veteran living in Tacoma, Washington. After his deployment, he struggled with suicidal ideations, which hindered his reintegration into civilian life. His isolation was compounded by mental barriers, such as the belief that "I'm weak," and strained relationships, particularly with his wife, often sparked by dinner arguments. His days were quiet, and his home felt like a refuge, yet his mind replayed the horrors of combat. The trauma had a tight grip on him, stalling his career ambitions and connections with others. As a Latino man, he faced stereotypes associated with "macho" behavior, which made him reluctant to seek help. He avoided VA support groups and suffered in silence. During one particularly difficult therapy session, he withdrew and clenched his hands in frustration.

However, he eventually participated in an ERF activity during session, a supportive space for veterans. There, he courageously shared his story about his deployment, the lingering terrors, and the strain on his family relationships. I helped him with goal setting using the ERF, where he identified his barriers and created a support map.

His session consisted of sharing his struggles, fostering a sense of therapeutic rapport. Carlos experienced a breakthrough when he set job goals using "win chains" to track his progress, which helped reduce his isolation. Now, he actively helps other Veterans through daily check-ins, transforming his personal victory into a legacy of brotherhood. Carlos's story illustrates how education can serve as a vital lifeline and a central theme in overcoming adversity.

ERF Practical Application Solutions:

- **Victory Legacy Affirm:** Affirm "My victory builds my legacy," using Black Feminist Theory to honor Black women's power, shifting isolation to connected veteran leadership.
- **Barrier Release Anchor:** Anchor with "barrier releases," applying Trauma-Informed Care Theory to ease mental hold, helping Black women claim their birthright to barrier-free thriving.
- **Reintegration Resilience Chain:** Chain supports for goals (e.g., "Weekly ally check"), drawing on Academic Resilience Theory to build grit, empowering Black women to turn shifts into legacy victories.

Research-Based Insight: The Proven Path to Thriving

The ERF, as a proven framework from the SLR, CP, and PAP, shows mindset shifts and advocacy counter trauma's effects—depression, overachievement—especially for Black women (Bertaux & Anderson, 2001; Gillum, 2019). The SLR's highlight survival mode's toll, with cultural pressures amplifying burnout (Erving et al., 2021; Hamilton-Mason et al., 2009). The CP's ERF integrates Black Feminist Theory to foster identity reconstruction, while Trauma-Informed Care Theory, per SAMHSA (2014), promotes safe healing spaces, reducing fatigue (Hauff et al., 2017). The PAP's workshop proves cultural rituals enhance resilience, breaking cycles (Hooks, 1981; Xu, 2024). The introduction notes education's role in thriving, with the conclusion calling for longitudinal studies to refine strategies (Luthar et al., 2000; O'Shea & Stone, 2014). The ERF empowers Black women and all professionals to turn survival into thriving legacies.

Practical Strategies: Steps to Thrive

From my capstone's PAP and 19 years of practice, these strategies shift you to thriving:

1. **Spot Survival Mode:** Identify stress signs (e.g., racing heart), as I do in therapy.
2. **Shift Mindsets:** Reframe doubts with affirmations, a client staple.
3. **Advocate Boldly:** Practice responses to bias, per my trainings.
4. **Use Cultural Healing:** Blend rituals like storytelling, as I guide.
5. **Take Action:** Set small goals, a method I teach.
6. **Build Support:** Map allies weekly, from the CP's focus.
7. **Celebrate Wins:** Journal one thrive moment daily, per the conclusion.

Your Thriving Spark

Choose one thriving act today—a bold word, a new ritual. I tell clients: thriving starts with one choice. Your spark starts now—claim your one thriving spark word for your epic legacy.

Activity Exercises: Embracing the Shift

1. **Thriving Checklist:** List growth habits.
2. **Affirmation Practice:** Write three resilient affirmations.
3. **Action Plan:** Set one thriving goal.
4. **Cultural Ritual:** Plan one healing practice.

Reflection Prompts:
1. What does thriving look like for you?
2. When do you find yourself in survival mode, and how can you shift out of it?
3. What affirmation lifts your spirits?
4. How can you advocate for yourself this week?
5. What cultural practice helps ground you?
6. When did you experience thriving, and how can you replicate that?
7. How can you encourage a colleague to thrive?
8. What is one bold step you can take toward thriving?

Final Reflection Question: How can you model thriving for my professional network?

CHAPTER 8: Legacy and Leadership

"Leadership isn't a title—it's the legacy you etch in hearts and horizons." – Dr. Lila Elliott

Graduation Day: Surrounded by my fellow doctoral colleagues from the UK, I hand out ERF ink pens. Mrs. Lewis, a former doctoral student who is now a mental health clinician, wrote with hers daily, saying, "Your ERF saved my first client." Tyrone, who was once skeptical, used my pen and shared, "I use the ERF pen for parenting with my children, Dr. Elliott, and it works." Legacy isn't just a title; it's the sound of the ink pen clicking as others carry the torch forward. I popped a piece of bubblegum, marking the end of my thoughts. The baton has been passed by Dr. Lila Effect™ | Architect of Legacy™.

Leading for Generations

My life's work in healing and teaching has taught me that leadership is ultimately about legacy. As a Black woman, I transformed my pain into advocacy at Riverside, mentoring colleagues at UK, guiding veterans at the VA, and shaping students at UK, all while developing my doctoral capstone. I remember those late nights, with incomplete thoughts piling up inside my brain, fueled by the desire to create something meaningful for my community, who face trauma and systemic barriers. Whether you are a Black woman in a school, supervisor, health care provider, mental health provider, executive leadership, parent, role model, life coach, or an international speaker. This chapter employs the ERF to convert healing into mentorship and systemic change, connecting professionals with the passion and strength of Black women at the core. Let's work to leave legacies that endure beyond our time.

Amara's Classroom Legacy (High School)

Amara successfully navigated bias and systemic inequities that challenged her leadership during high school.

Amara, a 41-year-old Black high school principal in Atlanta, comes from a family of teachers. She has confronted bias throughout her career, facing skepticism when her ideas were labeled as "too focused on race." Systemic inequities, such as underfunding, have undermined her leadership and contributed to low morale among her staff. Her days are filled with challenges, including budget cuts, and her office is cluttered with rejected proposals. This constant struggle has drained her spirit, compounded by stereotypes that portray her as "aggressive."

Amara grapples with a double bind, which intensifies her exhaustion and raises doubts about her impact on Black students. As a Black woman, she feels pressure to prove herself, which makes her advocacy efforts feel risky. Many late nights are spent strategizing alone. During one budget meeting, her proposal was rejected, leaving her feeling defeated amidst the chaos of papers scattered across her desk. In search of support, Amara joined my ERF conference, a space for educators to share their experiences. There, she "gave examples" about the biases she has faced in her career and the heavy burdens they create. I helped her navigate mentorship by centering cultural pride and shared goals. The group, which included diverse principals, connected over their shared challenges, creating a sense of legacy among them.

Amara's breakthrough came when she began mentoring teachers and advocating for equity funding using compelling data. She implemented "legacy checks" in her practice to inspire her team, effectively transforming her school into a beacon of empowerment. Ultimately, Amara's legacy has become a powerful model for Black principals.

ERF Practical Application Solutions:

- **Leadership Legacy Affirm:** Affirm "My leadership etches legacies," using Black Feminist Theory to honor Black women's power, shifting exhaustion to inspired high school leadership.
- **Inequity Release Ritual:** Release with "inequity sweeps," applying Trauma-Informed Care Theory to ease doubt, helping Black women claim their birthright to equity legacies.
- **Advocacy Resilience Ladder:** Ladder advocacy goals (e.g., "Weekly funding push"), drawing on Academic Resilience Theory to build grit, empowering Black women to turn bias into legacy classrooms.

Tom's Finance Footprint (Finance)

Tom observed inequalities within the team, and his inability to recognize these biases weakened both morale and leadership.

Tom is a 50-year-old white investment banker on Wall Street, coming from a finance dynasty. He observed significant inequalities within his team, particularly regarding Black and Latina staff who were often overlooked for promotions.

However, his lack of awareness of these biases made him hesitant to address the issue, ultimately weakening morale and leadership within the office. The atmosphere in his glass tower of an office was tense, and meetings felt awkward due to unspoken divides. His privilege clouded his judgment, leaving him unaware of the real problems.

This unawareness not only caused division among his teams but also led to his own self-doubt. He spent late nights reviewing performance reports, trying to avoid difficult conversations. One performance review underscored the high turnover rate, making Tom feel accountable for the situation. His desk was cluttered with notes reflecting his concern. To seek improvement, he joined my ERF continuing education units (CEU's), a supportive space for finance professionals.

During the sessions, he shared his experiences and acknowledged that his privilege had blinded him to others' struggles. I guided him and the group in exploring allyship through the ERF, fostering collaboration driven by shared goals. The diverse group of bankers discussed their challenges, which led to meaningful change.

Tom's breakthrough came when he decided to launch a diversity fund and began mentoring Black interns, holding weekly check-ins to provide guidance and support. He implemented "equity checks" in his practice to amplify underrepresented voices, transforming his firm into a legacy of inclusion. Tom's efforts have set a standard for finance leaders to follow.

ERF Practical Application Solutions:

- **Footprint Legacy Affirm:** Affirm "My footprint builds legacies," using Black Feminist Theory to honor Black women's power, shifting blindness to inclusive finance leadership.
- **Veil Release Anchor:** Anchor with "veil releases," applying Trauma-Informed Care Theory to ease doubt, helping Black women claim their birthright to veil-free teams.
- **Morale Goal Chain:** Chain team actions for equity (e.g., "Weekly ally share"), drawing on Academic Resilience Theory to build grit, empowering Black women to turn inequities into legacy footprints.

Mila's Therapy Trail (Private Practice)

Mila utilized the ERF to assist Latinx clients, addressing language barriers that limited both the effectiveness of the support and the clients' morale.

Mila is a 36-year-old Mexican American therapist in San Antonio who follows a healing tradition. She used the ERF to guide her Latinx clients, but language barriers, specifically the lack of English-only resources, limited her impact, leading to frustration and low morale in her practice. Her days were filled with struggles around translation, her office cluttered with untranslated handouts, and her spirit drained by her clients' unmet needs.

The challenges she faced were due to systemic gaps, which amplified her doubt as a Latina healer. She spent late nights researching and often avoided team discussions. As a Latina woman, she encountered stereotypes such as "not being professional enough," which made advocacy for her clients more difficult. One client struggled with the materials available, and Mila felt ineffective, leaving her confidence shaken. To find support, Mila joined my ERF group, a space designed for therapists to share their experiences. There, she "reveals" about her journey; the call of her healing tradition and the barriers she faced. I guided the group in advocating for culturally relevant resources, emphasizing the importance of cultural pride and bilingual tools.

The group, made up of diverse therapists, shared their struggles, creating a supportive community. Mila's breakthrough came when she began advocating for bilingual services, inspiring her team through monthly discussions. In her practice, she implemented "pride trails" to foster connections with her clients, transforming her practice into a legacy of accessible healing. Mila's journey became a beacon of hope for other Latina therapists, showing that cultural pride and accessibility can coexist in the healing process.

ERF Practical Application Solutions:

- **Trail Legacy Affirm**: Affirm "My trail etches my legacy," using Black Feminist Theory to honor Black women's power, shifting gaps to inclusive therapy leadership.

- **Gap Release Ritual:** Release with "gap rituals" that apply Trauma-Informed Care Theory to ease frustration and help Black women claim their birthright to gap-free healing.
- **Impact Resilience Chain:** Chain advocacy actions (e.g., "Weekly resource push"), drawing on Academic Resilience Theory to build grit, empowering Black women to turn barriers into legacy trails.

Keisha's Salon Legacy (Community Hub)

Keisha transformed her salon into a hub, but the emotional weight of her clients' stories left her questioning her role.

Keisha is a 33-year-old Black stylist based in Harlem who has dedicated her salon to serving the community. However, the emotional toll of listening to her clients' stories, which often reflect her own trauma from losing family members, has left her questioning her purpose. This emotional drain has contributed to her feelings of fatigue and low self-worth. Her daily routine is filled with styling hair; braids and blowouts, while clients share their grief, often reminding Keisha of her own loss, particularly the passing of her mother.

She experiences physical manifestations of this stress, like back tension, and finds herself in quiet moments of self-doubt. The burden of others' trauma has dulled her passion for her work.

As a Black woman, Keisha also encounters stereotypes that label her simply as "just a stylist," which amplifies her struggles. Late nights spent cleaning the salon are often accompanied by her desire to avoid deep conversations that might bring her emotions to the surface. One day, a client's story of loss struck a chord with Keisha, causing her hands to tremble as her own grief resurfaced.

In search of support, Keisha attended my ERF talk, a space designed for professionals in the field. There, she shared her experiences of family loss and the weight of her responsibilities. I facilitated mentorship using the ERF framework, focusing on cultural pride and the importance of telling shared stories. The group, composed of diverse stylists, "had a dialogue" about their own pains, allowing them to create a legacy rooted in mutual support.

Keisha's breakthrough came when she began mentoring young Black women, focusing on resilience and empowerment. In her salon, she implemented "pride shares" to recharge her spirit, transforming her business into a beacon of community upliftment and legacy. Through her journey, Keisha has become a source of inspiration for those around her.

ERF Practical Application Solutions:

- **Hub Legacy Affirm:** Affirm "My hub builds my legacy," using Black Feminist Theory to honor Black women's power, shifting drain to vibrant salon leadership.
- **Drain Release Anchor:** Anchor with "drain releases," applying Trauma-Informed Care Theory to ease emotional load, helping Black women claim their birthright to energized hubs.
- **Uplift Goal Chain:** Chain clients for uplifts (e.g., "Weekly share"), drawing on Academic Resilience Theory to build grit, empowering Black women to turn doubt into legacy hubs.

Research-Based Insight: The Proven Call of Leadership

Leadership in the ERF extends resilience into actionable influence. Drawing from the SLR, CP, and PAP, Black Feminist Theory and Academic Resilience Theory

99

illustrate how mentorship, advocacy, and culturally informed guidance position Black women as agents of systemic transformation (Hill Collins, 2000; Martin & Marsh, 2006). The SLR's 20 studies show mentorship bridges gaps in educational and professional landscapes, reducing mental health disparities (Bertaux & Anderson, 2001; Moorosi et al., 2018). The CP's ERF emphasizes cultural identity as a leadership strength, while the PAP's workshop proves systemic advocacy enhances outcomes (Hauff et al., 2017; SAMHSA, 2014). The notes of education's role in breaking cycles, with the conclusion calling for policy reforms to support Black women's leadership (Hooks, 1981; Xu, 2024). The capstone advocates longitudinal studies to refine strategies, empowering Black women and all professionals to etch legacies in hearts and horizons (Gillum, 2019; Chance, 2022).

Practical Strategies: Crafting Your Legacy

From my capstone's PAP, these strategies craft your legacy:

1. **Advocate Boldly:** Push for policy changes.
2. **Mentor Generously**: Share skills with others, a client tactic.
3. **Drive Systemic Change:** Use advocacy tools.
4. **Celebrate Education:** Promote learning as legacy.
5. **Set Legacy Goals:** Plan your impact.
6. **Build Allies:** Map support networks weekly.
7. **Reflect Impact:** Journal one legacy act daily, per the conclusion.

Your Legacy Seed

Plant a legacy today: be a mentor, advocate, or inspire at least one person. I tell clients: your legacy starts now. Your seed starts now; watch it grow.

Activity Exercises: Etching Your Mark

1. **Legacy Letter:** Write to a younger person about the lessons you've learned.
2. **Impact Plan:** Outline three contributions.
3. **Vision Board:** Create a legacy vision.
4. **Advocacy Action:** Plan one step for systemic change

Reflection Prompts:
1. What legacy do you want to leave behind?
2. Who can you mentor this week?
3. What systemic change can you advocate for?
4. How has your healing journey inspired others?
5. What is one bold leadership action you can take?
6. When did you feel like a leader, and what contributed to that feeling?
7. How can you share your story to uplift others?
8. What is one step you can take today to work towards your legacy?

Final Reflection Question: What will be your one act of legacy today?

Acknowledgement
The Victory Lap Shout-Out

Look, if God had not said RISE, I would still be folded in a chair. Thank you, Lord, for the storms that taught flight, the nights that taught fire, the scars that spell the story.

To my parents, Jerome & Betty Bethea: the original Architects. Sugar Momma's hands were small but powerful hands that turned into forgiveness and love; Daddy's hustle spelled impossible backward. I am your living blueprint and proud as hell to be your daughter.

To Walter, Joseph, and Bonita, the Code-9, always on speed dial. You were drivers, bail money, and backup parents, an unlicensed therapist, best friends, and "all we got crew." I love y'all sideways and straight.

To Donye "My Heartbeat" Elliott, my soulmate, now my administrative assistant, a 9-live survivor (and I mean it too-you are a walking miracle) with "the patience of Job" and the jokes of Kevin Hart. You held the flashlight while I drafted; now we are both glowing. Thank you for being my RIB.

To Jhaydon & Jayshawn, thank you two for being my co-authors. Jhaydon for editing my fears, Jayshawn for illustrating my joy, and let me not forget my furry son Ghost, the 138-pound rottweiler who growled at deadlines like they were intruders in our home. Ghost, you win, good boy.

To Rise2Write Publishing, you took my bubblegum wrappers and gave them a binding. You said, "Just write," when I said, "I want it to be PERFECT." Grateful for my publisher, Rise2Write, which does not cut it, so let me personally say, "Thank you so much, Dee."

To my family, friends, colleagues, and every mentor who poured tea into me with knowledge instead of actual tea, you shaped clay until I fit my own mold. And to every reader holding this. Yeah, you. You are the next signature on the legacy wall. Boom. Dr. Lila Elliott, also known as the Dr. Lila Effect™ | Architect of Legacy™. Because gratitude is not a footnote; it is the fireworks after the finish line.

Thank you for your support,
Dr. Lila Elliott

References

Bertaux, N. E., & Anderson, M. C. (2001). An emerging tradition of educational achievement: African American women in college and the professions, 1920–1950. *Equity & Excellence in Education, 34*(2), 16–21. https://doi.org/10.1080/1066568010340203

Chance, N. L. (2022). Resilient leadership: A phenomenological exploration into how Black women in higher education leadership navigate cultural adversity. *Journal of Humanistic Psychology, 62*(1), 44–78. https://doi.org/10.1177/00221678211003000

Erving, C. L., Satcher, L. A., & Chen, Y. (2021). Psychologically resilient, but physically vulnerable? Exploring the psychosocial determinants of African American women's mental and physical health. *Sociology of Race and Ethnicity, 7*(1), 116–133. https://doi.org/10.1177/2332649219900284

Gillum, T. L. (2019). African American survivors of intimate partner violence: Lived experience and future directions for research. *Journal of Aggression, Maltreatment & Trauma, 30*(6), 731–748. https://doi.org/10.1080/10926771.2019.1607962

Hamilton-Mason, J., Hall, J. C., & Everett, J. E. (2009). And Some of Us Are Braver: Stress and Coping Among African American Women. *Journal of Human Behavior in the Social Environment, 19*(5), 463–482. https://doi.org/10.1080/10911350902832142

Hill Collins, P. (2000). *Black feminist thought: Knowledge, consciousness, and the politics of empowerment* (2nd ed.). Routledge. https://doi.org/10.4324/9780203900055

Martin, A. J., & Marsh, H. W. (2006). Academic resilience and its psychological and educational correlates: A construct validity approach. *Psychology in the Schools, 43*(3), 267–281. https://doi.org/10.1002/pits.20149

Moorosi, P., Fuller, K., & Reilly, E. (2018). Leadership and intersectionality: Constructions of successful leadership among Black women school principals in three different contexts. *Management in Education, 32*(4), 152–159. https://doi.org/10.1177/0892020618791006

O'Shea, S., & Stone, C. (2014). The hero's journey: Stories of women returning to education. *International Journal of the First Year in Higher Education, 5*(1), 79–91. https://doi.org/10.5204/intjfyhe.v5i1.186

Substance Abuse and Mental Health Services Administration. (2014). *SAMHSA's concept of trauma and guidance for a trauma-informed approach* (HHS Publication No. SMA 14-4884). https://library.samhsa.gov/sites/default/files/sma14-4884.pdf

ABOUT THE AUTHOR

Dr. Lila Elliott, a 19-year seasoned federal government employee, has transformed lives with unyielding passion, earning her Doctor of Social Work (Summa Cum Laude) from the University of Kentucky (UK). From working in Suicide Prevention at the Veterans Affairs, to being an inpatient psych therapist at Riverside Mental Health and Recovery Center, to educating and shaping brilliant minds at UK as a Professor, she is a beacon light for Black women reclaiming power from trauma. Her Empowerment and Resilience Framework (ERF), born from her doctoral research, fuses Black Feminist Theory, Trauma-Informed Care Theory, and Academic Resilience Theory to heal and empower. With elite certifications in Eye Movement Desensitization and Reprocessing (EMDR) Therapy, Dialectical Behavior Therapy (DBT), and Trauma Yoga, Dr. Lila's led groundbreaking programs, mentored future leaders, and spoken globally, earning accolades like Woman of the Year 2025. Her manual, Unleashing

Empowerment and Resilience, is a clarion call for professionals, educators, corporate leaders, therapists, and community builders to turn pain into purpose. It's a lifeline for Black women and all seeking to architect legacies of strength. Connect at www.thedrlilaeffect.com for an interest in booking future consultation, speaking engagements, architect lab trainings, and/or coaching needs.